Deceptions

Paul Wheeler

A SAMUEL FRENCH ACTING EDITION

FOUNDED 1830

SAMUELFRENCH.COM
SAMUELFRENCH-LONDON.CO.UK

FOR PRODUCTION ENQUIRIES

UNITED STATES AND CANADA

Info@SamuelFrench.com

1-866-598-8449

UNITED KINGDOM AND EUROPE

Theatre@SamuelFrench-London.co.uk

020-7255-4302

Each title is subject to availability from Samuel French, depending upon
country of performance. Please be aware that *DECEPTIONS* may not be
licensed by Samuel French in your territory. Professional and amateur
producers should contact the nearest Samuel French office or licensing
partner to verify availability.

MUSIC USE NOTE

Licensees are solely responsible for obtaining formal written permission from copyright owners to use copyrighted music in the performance of this play and are strongly cautioned to do so. If no such permission is obtained by the licensee, then the licensee must use only original music that the licensee owns and controls. Licensees are solely responsible and liable for all music clearances and shall indemnify the copyright owners of the play(s) and their licensing agent, Samuel French, against any costs, expenses, losses and liabilities arising from the use of music by licensees. Please contact the appropriate music licensing authority in your territory for the rights to any incidental music.

IMPORTANT BILLING AND CREDIT REQUIREMENTS

If you have obtained performance rights to this title, please refer to your licensing agreement for important billing and credit requirements.

Deceptions premiered at the King's Head Theatre
in London in February, 1991, produced by Ian
Fricker for Excalibur Productions, and directed by
Mark Rayment, it had the following cast:

Julia Smythe...........................Anna Carteret

Adrian Wainwright.....................Jamie Glover

CHARACTERS

JULIA SMYTHE, a psychiatrist in her early forties.

ADRIAN WAINWRIGHT, a young man of twenty-three.

The action takes place in Smythe's consulting rooms and in Wainwright's bedsitter.

DECEPTIONS

ACT I

Scene 1

The time is present, the place a psychiatrist's office somewhere in London; Mayfair perhaps, or the Harley street area of Marylebone. JULIA SMYTHE, a handsome woman in her early forties sits in a chair. Next to her is a side table where she has placed a large yellow notepad.

Lying on a chaise longue facing away from her is ADRIAN WAINWRIGHT, a young man in his early twenties.

JULIA can hardly be described as a person who stamps their personality on their surroundings. Apart from the chair she is seated in, the chaise longue, the side table and a desk, the room is blandly bare of intimate details; a diploma is framed on a wall and a small bookshelf contains a few volumes, but that's about it. A window looks out onto the facade of smart nineteenth-century terraced housing.

Calling JULIA handsome rather than attractive sums up the impression she gives to the observer. A smart suit, not exactly severe, is offset by a high-neck white ruffled blouse. Jewelry is at a minimum; tiny earrings, one ring on her right hand. Hair short and in place.

7

ADRIAN, on the other hand, is dressed in jeans and turtleneck sweater. His hair is longish and he wears a Zapata moustache. He looks like a leftover from the nineteen seventies.

SMYTHE. Tell me when you're ready.
ADRIAN. (*A wriggle to get comfortable.*) Ready.
SMYTHE. You say you've not done this before.
ADRIAN. No.
SMYTHE. You may feel a little self-conscious at first but that will soon pass.
ADRIAN. I want to cooperate. I really do.
SMYTHE. You're not here to cooperate. You're here to discuss.
ADRIAN. I'm sorry.
SMYTHE. Do you understand the difference?
ADRIAN. I don't have to agree with you all the time.
SMYTHE. You don't have to agree with me at all.
ADRIAN. Right. I mean, I understand.
SMYTHE. If I don't say much, you mustn't assume that I'm not listening.
ADRIAN. Right. I mean, fine.
SMYTHE. (*The hint of a smile.*) If you are happier saying "right," I won't take it that you're agreeing with me.
ADRIAN. Right. I mean fine. I mean O.K.
SMYTHE. Let's make a start.
ADRIAN. (*Tucking his hands behind his head and crossing his ankles.*) Ready when you are, Mr. DeMille.
SMYTHE. Sorry?
ADRIAN. Nothing—

SMYTHE. Nothing is "nothing" here. Everything is relevant. Why did you call me Mr. DeMille?

ADRIAN. It's stupid, really. There used to be a film director called Cecil B. DeMille.

SMYTHE. *(Begins to jot words down on the pad.)* Ah ... yes ...

ADRIAN. He specialized in biblical epics. There's an old story—I'm sure you know it—

SMYTHE. The *biblical* story, you mean—?

ADRIAN. No. The one that ends "Ready when you are, Mr. DeMille."

(A pause.)

SMYTHE. I'm getting a little confused ...

ADRIAN. *(Telling it fast, as if ashamed it is so corny and well known.)* Cecil B. DeMille was making a film about how Sodom and Gomorrah was destroyed—or some huge disaster like that. Anyway, he's spent zillions on a climax where there's a flood, an earthquake and a fire. So, to make sure there aren't any slip-ups he has four camera crews set up in different places to cover it. He shouts "Action!" and the special effects create the flood, then the earthquake and then the fire that brings everything down. When it's finished he calls up the first crew and says "Did you get it?" and they say: "Sorry, Mr. DeMille we forgot to load the film." He asks the second crew and they say: "Sorry, Mr. DeMille, the camera jammed." He calls the third lot and the cameraman there says "Sorry, Mr. DeMille, we lost the focus." Absolutely out of his mind he

rings the fourth crew and yells: "What about you guys?"
And they say: "Ready when you are, Mr. DeMille."

(A long pause follows as SMYTHE writes.)

ADRIAN. I don't think it really happened.
SMYTHE. Do you like the cinema?
ADRIAN. Love it. Films are a passion of mine.
Especially the old ones. I must have two hundred I've
videoed off the television. Cary Grant, Katherine Hepburn,
Cagney ... Bogart ... When I was at university I ran a film
society. It was the happiest time of my life. One term I
only showed films in which the actors had been awful. You
know what the English are like—they love it when famous
people fall on their arses—sorry—faces. I tell you, you
don't know what embarrassment is until you've seen
Humphrey Bogart play a homicidal painter in a film called
The Two Mrs. Carrolls. Or seen Clark Gable sing and
dance in—
SMYTHE. We may be leaping ahead a little—
ADRIAN. Sorry. Mention films and I'm away.
SMYTHE. Where do you live?
ADRIAN. At home.

(Pause.)

SMYTHE. With your parents?
ADRIAN. Yes.

(There follows another pause. SMYTHE wants him to continue but HE has nothing naturally to continue with.)

SMYTHE. Just keep talking. Say anything that comes into your head.

ADRIAN. Oh, right. Let's see—I live with my parents and my sister in Chelsea in a nineteen thirties house. With a garage at the back and a tiny garden in front. It's on three floors and my bedroom is in the rear where it's quieter although the neighbors, being French, make a lot of noise in the morning when they get their kids ready to go to the Lycée—

SMYTHE. *(Beginning to regret asking him to talk about anything he liked.)* Do you like living there?

ADRIAN. No. Not much. Not at all, in fact.

SMYTHE. Why not?

ADRIAN. I'm twenty-three. I'd like to have a place of my own.

SMYTHE. Why don't you move out?

ADRIAN. It's my mother.

SMYTHE. What about her?

ADRIAN. When I went away to college, she got very depressed. There's a name for it—when the children leave home—

SMYTHE. The Empty Nest Syndrome—

ADRIAN. That's it.

SMYTHE. What about your sister? Wasn't she there?

ADRIAN. They don't get on.

SMYTHE. Why not?

ADRIAN. They fell out when she reached thirteen. My sister became the ultimate pain in the neck. (*Mimics*.) "God, Mother, do you *seriously* expect me to wear something like *that!*" "Are you actually telling me I *can't* stay out till three in the morning, that I *can't* go riding on the back of Drongo's Harley Davidson ..."

SMYTHE. So your mother's depression was caused simply because *you* weren't at home.

ADRIAN. We've always been close.

SMYTHE. And you live there for her sake.

ADRIAN. (*Sighs.*) Yes.

(*SMYTHE writes at some length and a silence extends between them.*)

SMYTHE. What about your father?

ADRIAN. What about him?

SMYTHE. Isn't he an adequate companion for your mother?

ADRIAN. You'll have to ask her that.

SMYTHE. Have you talked to him about why you feel compelled to stay there?

ADRIAN. I tried once.

SMYTHE. What did he say?

ADRIAN. He didn't say anything. My father is a great nodder. He just nods his head when you talk of anything more consequential than the weather.

SMYTHE. (*Making more notes, turning a page.*) Tell me more about him.

ADRIAN. He's in his fifties, quite tall—

SMYTHE. No, I meant, do you get on?

ADRIAN. We don't actually come to blows. Anyway, he's mostly away. Either at the office or abroad. I don't see a lot of him.

SMYTHE. May I ask what kind of work he does?

ADRIAN. (*Pauses, then laughs quickly, as if just realizing something.*) Actually, no, you can't.

SMYTHE. Why?

ADRIAN. It's a state secret.

(HE laughs again, a little longer this time, enjoying the thought. SMYTHE is puzzled but tries not to show it.)

SMYTHE. Ah. I see ... (*SHE keeps writing.*)

ADRIAN. Hang on a sec. Aren't you sworn to secrecy about what goes on in here?

SMYTHE. Yes.

ADRIAN. That's all right, then. My father's a spy. He works for M.I. 6.

SMYTHE. (*Looks across at him sharply. Then covering up professionally.*) MmmHmmm ...

ADRIAN. Six covers foreign espionage and counter insurgency. Five is internal security. There're some other numbers, but nobody knows what they do. Keep an eye on Mars or flying saucers probably.

SMYTHE. Would it be fair to suggest that your father's reluctance to confide his thoughts to his family is possibly due to the confidential nature of his work?

ADRIAN. I haven't a clue. That's the kind of thing you people like to kick around, isn't it?

(A pause.)

SMYTHE. What I'm trying to establish, what I'm trying to isolate, is the reason why you continue to live at home when it clearly is making you unhappy. You say it's because your mother feels lonely and depressed without you. Your sister gives her no comfort nor, apparently does your father.

ADRIAN. (*Thinks about this for a moment, still facing away from her on the chaise longue.*) Mmmm. I see. You think my problem is somehow related to my living at home ...

SMYTHE. Perhaps.

ADRIAN. (*Thinks more on the idea which starts to animate him. HE smiles, wraps his arms around himself and appears fascinated by the suggestion.*) You know, you could be right. I'd never thought of that before.

SMYTHE. Now wait. We've only just touched on one possibility—

(*But HE is now in the grip of a heady revelation. HE stands up, his face beaming with pleasure.*)

ADRIAN. The fact that I've been living only to please my *mother*—my own mother is the reason why I'm miserable—so *therefore*, it's because of *her* that I became impotent! Yes!!

SMYTHE. (*Puts down her pen in concern at Adrian's escalating flight of fancy.*) We've hardly scratched the surface. Please, sit down. You mustn't assume that the first idea we find to discuss is the definitive answer to your problem—

ADRIAN. (*But HE is not listening. HE beams radiantly as HE paces the room.*) It's absolutely fantastic! My friends all said I was wasting money coming to a shrink to find out why I couldn't get it up. But I think I've cracked it! In ten minutes flat! I'm cured!

SMYTHE. I don't *cure* people. My function is to treat someone so they—

ADRIAN. (*But in his ecstasy HE cuts her off. HE thrusts a hand into his pocket.*) I'm getting a reaction already. My God, I can feel energy surging inside me! I'm going to tell everyone you're an absolute miracle worker—

SMYTHE. (*Very irritated now.*) You'll do nothing of the kind—

ADRIAN. (*Takes his hand from his pocket.*) What I'll do is this. I'll nip round right now and see my girl friend. If it doesn't work, I'll come back and we'll try and think of something else—(*HE takes out a wallet.*)

ADRIAN. Do I pay the girl outside? How much it is, by the way?

SMYTHE. I can't stop you leaving, of course, but I strongly advise you to do nothing until we've spoken further. (*SHE sits back and folds her arms, fixing him with a reproving look.*)

ADRIAN. What about?

SMYTHE. Please sit down.

(*HE pauses, shrugs and sits—not lies—down on the chaise longue.*)

SMYTHE. (*Gathers herself, picks up the pen and poised over the notepad:*) This girl friend you mentioned.

ADRIAN. Anna.

SMYTHE. (*Making a note.*) How long have you known her?

ADRIAN. About a year.

SMYTHE. And you had normal relations before your difficulties began?

ADRIAN. Did we have it off, you mean?

SMYTHE. Yes.

ADRIAN. Oh, yes. Yes, we had a pretty wild sex life. She was very keen.

SMYTHE. She wanted to make love frequently.

ADRIAN. All the time. She once made me do it in the cinema.

SMYTHE. Did that worry you?

ADRIAN. Well, it was pretty empty at the time and we were on the back row—but the usherettes kept dashing back and forth behind us—

SMYTHE. No, I meant—did making love in a public place *offend* you?

ADRIAN. Not offend, no. I thought it was rather bold of her. But she's like that. (*Mimics a foreign accent.*) "Oh, you tightup Englishmen! Vy you not let yourselfs go once in a vile ...?"

SMYTHE. She isn't English, I take it.

ADRIAN. She's Polish.

SMYTHE. (*More notes, a pause.*) And so you maintained a vigorous sex life with Anna until you became unable to achieve an erection?

ADRIAN. Well, that *did* put a bit of a damper on things.

SMYTHE. (*Continues to write rather a lot.*) And what does Anna say about your present—er—incapacity?

ADRIAN. As you might imagine, she's mightily pissed off.

SMYTHE. Has she threatened to end the relationship?

ADRIAN. Oh no. Not at all. But she's taken it personally. You know, she thinks it's *her*. I told her of course it isn't.

SMYTHE. How did she respond to that?

ADRIAN. She wanted to know how I could be sure. Had I tried anyone else?

SMYTHE. And have you?

ADRIAN. (*A pause, a fidget.*) Once.

SMYTHE. Ah ... (*More writing.*)

ADRIAN. Look, I simply wanted to find out what had gone wrong. So, one night, I picked up one of the girls in Shepherd's Market. That's a place in Mayfair where prostitutes hang out—

SMYTHE. I'm aware of the area—

ADRIAN. But it was no good. She tried everything. It cost me a bomb.

SMYTHE. (*After more writing.*) It's lasted how long now, your detumescence?

ADRIAN. De-tumescence? Christ, you make me sound like a compost heap.

SMYTHE. Your—condition.

ADRIAN. Six months.

SMYTHE. And throughout this time, Anna has been supportive.

ADRIAN. She's been wonderful.

SMYTHE. Do you know if she's remained faithful to you?

ADRIAN. I don't know.

SMYTHE. Would you be angry if she hadn't?

ADRIAN. I wouldn't *like* it very much. But I could hardly be *angry*. I mean, it isn't her fault. I think I'd probably find someone else. Just for sex, I'm talking about. For relief. I wouldn't *dump* her just because we couldn't make love.

SMYTHE. There's always masturbation.

ADRIAN. There's *always* masturbation. But it isn't the same as hanging onto some throbbing alive feminine creature, smelling of Fendi and hair conditioner. You don't work up much of a sweat whacking it about in the bath. I rather used to like the *aroma* of sex.

SMYTHE. You never felt—threatened—by her constant demands?

ADRIAN. *Threatened?*

SMYTHE. Worried that you could not satisfy her. After all, a man's performance is limited. A woman's isn't. Sometimes he may feel he is inadequate, especially with someone possessing a libido like Anna's. He may think he is being unfavorably compared to other men. And this could lead to a temporary impotence.

ADRIAN. (*Looks across at her, starting to frown.*) Hang on. I thought you said my mother was the reason—

SMYTHE. I said nothing of the sort—

ADRIAN. Now you reckon it's *Anna's* fault—?

SMYTHE. Wait a minute. I want you to listen to me. My role is not to blame anyone. I am merely trying to find possible causes.

ADRIAN. Well, that's two you've come up with. How many more are there?

SMYTHE. (*Detects the frostiness in his voice and puts down her pen.*) This isn't a garage. I'm not a mechanic.

ADRIAN. Aren't you? I thought people came here to get patched up. You're a doctor. Your job is to cure them, isn't it?

SMYTHE. Not in the ordinary sense of the word—I *treat* them—in the end they cure themselves—

ADRIAN. Now hold on a sec. You have patients. Right? They come in saying they think they're a stick of rhubarb, and you convince them they aren't. Isn't that how it goes?

SMYTHE. (*Offended by the reference, and it shows.*) Horticulture is not my speciality.

ADRIAN. All right. They think they're Napoleon—

SMYTHE. You're taking extreme cases and assuming they are the norm. Most of my clients are people like you. They have something on their mind. They don't feel confident. I try and help.

ADRIAN. For a fee.

SMYTHE. I have some specific qualifications that enable me to advise. That's what they pay for.

ADRIAN. But if you *don't* cure them, you still take their money.

SMYTHE. I've explained, I don't profess to effect a cure.

ADRIAN. I paid that whore to make me feel confident again and she also had specific qualifications. A hell of a lot of them.

SMYTHE. And she failed.

ADRIAN. Yes—
SMYTHE. Did she return your money?

(HE doesn't answer. SHE waits, with the faintest of smiles, until HE stops fidgeting.)

SMYTHE. I don't wish to encourage the notion that my function is similar to that of a prostitute, but I agree we are both paid to reduce mental tension whether we succeed or not.
ADRIAN. You are both strangers who are paid to sort out problems. The only difference is, she's faster. I've heard some people go to psychiatrists for years.
SMYTHE. That's true.
ADRIAN. Which means you don't do as good a job as your average tart.
SMYTHE. (*A pause. SHE plays with her pen.*) I'm aware you have begun to adopt a certain aggression toward my question.
ADRIAN. (*Stands again.*) You shouldn't have asked me to stay.
SMYTHE. You still have ten minutes left—(*SHE picks up her wrist watch which is propped with the face towards her on the desk.*)
ADRIAN. I don't care about the time!
SMYTHE. Tell me why you feel anger.
ADRIAN. I'll tell you why I feel anger, as you quaintly put it. I feel anger because you kicked off by giving me a reason for my impotence that I hadn't thought of. It never occurred to me the answer might be because of my mother. But now you switch and say Anna could be the cause. Well

of *course* she could be! Do you think *I* hadn't thought of that? You don't think I hadn't wondered whether there is a finite number of times the penis can perform the act of congress? That once it reaches its limit, it pops its clogs like anything else? Like a pump or a—a coffee percolator? They just wear out like other organs. Eyes dim, ears stop hearing, why not the poor old chopper? That much, doctor, is obvious. And I didn't come here to listen to *obvious* suggestions why I'm unable at present to have a stiffy.

SMYTHE. What other obvious suggestions do you have in mind?

ADRIAN. Who's paying who here? *You're* the one with the "special qualifications"—

SMYTHE. All right, give me a suggestion.

ADRIAN. (*Makes an exasperated gesture and paces about the room around her.*) All right, if it's games you want—I'm surprised you haven't already come up with the one that goes— "perhaps I am basically homosexual."

SMYTHE. (*A pause. SMYTHE looks at him calmly.*) I see. So this idea *has* occurred to you.

ADRIAN. (*Makes an exasperated grimace at the ceiling.*) I don't believe it!

SMYTHE. Despite your impatience with the system, I have to explore *all* avenues of enquiry, obvious or not.

ADRIAN. O.K. Maybe I'm homosexual. So, throughout the time when I was in bed with Anna—or even in the back row of the Chelsea Cannon—you're saying that I was really thinking about Nigel.

SMYTHE. (*Picking up the pen.*) Who's Nigel?

ADRIAN. A figure of *speech* ,for Christ's sake!

SMYTHE. Does the thought of being homosexual increase your anger?

ADRIAN. Yes. Frankly ...

SMYTHE. Why?

ADRIAN. Because, doctor, I happen to *like* the presence of women. I like their perfume. I am baffled by their thought processes. They are so alien to those of men. They're fascinating to the extent that it's not unusual for me to spend a sleepless night trying to figure them out. I like the subtle way women flirt. I respond to their voices, their laughter when they are happy, their sympathy when I'm ill or depressed. I love their thoughtfulness, the appropriate gift for a birthday or a thank you for having had a nice time. If I am to be homosexual, then I'm going to have to exchange these delights for the company of hairy chested buffoons, all projecting a body odor that would stun an elephant, whose idea of a good night out is to smash beer cans against their foreheads and bet one another they can't belch heir way through the alphabet.

(There follows a long pause while SMYTHE calmly finishes her notes and ADRIAN perches his backside on her desk watching her. When she has finished:)

SMYTHE. I'm struck by the number of times that olfactory references occur in your conversation. The sense of smell seems to play a prominent part in your life.

ADRIAN. (*Annoyed at her coolness, picks up her watch.*) You really are going to insist on doing the full session, aren't you—?

SMYTHE. Do you have a job?

ADRIAN. I work in a fruit and vegetable store.

SMYTHE. Oh—(*SHE writes.*)

ADRIAN. You're surprised.

SMYTHE. No—

ADRIAN. Admit it. You're surprised. Outwardly you're calm, professionally inscrutable, but inwardly you're very surprised to hear I work in a greengrocers'.

SMYTHE. "Surprise" is too strong a word—

ADRIAN. No, it's not, it's quite mild. Nothing comes lower than surprise. First, you're surprised, then you're astonished, then amazed, then flabbergasted, then—maybe thunderstruck.

SMYTHE. Very well, I'm surprised.

ADRIAN. Because I went to university, because my father works for M.I. 6 and because I speak properly and live in an expensive house, you find it inconceivable that I should sell vegetables.

SMYTHE. It is certainly not inconceivable. These days it isn't even unlikely.

(*ADRIAN is caught by a thought that makes him walk very slowly across the room and back again.*)

SMYTHE. What's the matter?

ADRIAN. I'm just thinking what you said.

SMYTHE. About what?

ADRIAN. My constant referring to smell. I'd never realized that before.

SMYTHE. You see how useful it can be to broaden the scope of our investigations?

ADRIAN. Shall I tell you my chief job at the store?

SMYTHE. If you want to.

ADRIAN. I have to get up at five in the morning, drive down to the wholesale market and buy our daily supply.

SMYTHE. (*Not particularly aroused.*) Really ...

ADRIAN. Do you know how that's done? The choosing, I mean.

SMYTHE. Tell me.

ADRIAN. What do you do when you buy fresh fruit?

SMYTHE. I—er—I don't know. I never buy it.

ADRIAN. Never?

SMYTHE. Tell me what happens when you buy fresh fruit.

ADRIAN. (*Cups his hands and brings them to his nose.*) You smell it.

SMYTHE. (*SHE makes a note.*) Of course.

ADRIAN. I'm alarmed to hear you don't buy fruit.

SMYTHE. Do you like your work?

ADRIAN. All the experts nowadays tell you to cut down on red meat and eat more fresh fruit and vegetables. I'm surprised you, a doctor, don't know that—

SMYTHE. Do you enjoy your work?

ADRIAN. (*Thoughtfully.*) Do I enjoy it?

SMYTHE. Yes. Do you like buying at the market every morning?

ADRIAN. (*Pauses and paces, thinking further.*) Yes. Yes, I do. I have to, don't I, to get up at five o'clock each day. (*HE falls silent.*)

SMYTHE. Tell me what you're thinking—

ADRIAN. Look, I'm sorry I was rude just now.

SMYTHE. That doesn't matter.

ADRIAN. I'm beginning to realize what you mean about having to ask a wide range of questions. It's all starting to fit together.

SMYTHE. In what way?

(Adrian sits heavily on the edge of the chaise longue. HE looks vulnerable, anxious.)

SMYTHE. What seems to be fitting together?

ADRIAN. For some time I've had a feeling, very vague, almost subconscious feeling that my attitude at work has been going through a kind of change. You've managed to bring it into focus.

SMYTHE. What kind of change?

ADRIAN. Look, I know this sounds absolutely ridiculous, but when I was going strong with Anna, I used to love to buy figs.

SMYTHE. Figs?

ADRIAN. They let you taste fruit first to make sure they're ripe. I used to like to take a soft ripe fig and—Well, you know how you eat them—

SMYTHE. No, I don't. Tell me.

ADRIAN. Well, you split them open, bring them up to your mouth and with your tongue you kind of nibble at the insides—

(HE mimes this and the implication becomes clear to SMYTHE.)

SMYTHE. I see.

ADRIAN. When I ate a fig, I though of Anna. I thought of women.

SMYTHE. (*Makes a note.*) I see.

ADRIAN. (*Takes his hands from his mouth and looks nervous and pulls a pained look.*) But I've just realized, since Anna and I stopped making love, since women no longer turn me on, I've—Jesus, doctor, you've just made me aware of something—

SMYTHE. Aware of what?

ADRIAN. I don't have any interest in figs any longer. Now—

SMYTHE. Now what? Go on—

ADRIAN. Gradually, over the last few months, I've become increasingly obsesses with —bananas—

SMYTHE. (*Making rapid notes.*) In what way, obsessed?

ADRIAN. Look, you don't have to taste a banana to see if it's ripe. You can tell by the color. But every morning, I—I take one from the stall—I—peel it slowly and —oh, Doctor, you're right, I must be turning homosexual—I hold it to my mouth. My lips gently curl over—over the end and—oh my *God*!

(*His miming ends and HE covers his face. SMYTHE waits, pen poised. Then her watch ALARM goes off and SHE impatiently stops it.*)

ADRIAN. (*Slowly takes his hands away from his face. HE is smiling broadly.*) Made it.

SMYTHE. Made what?

ADRIAN. (*Stands, picks up his jacket, still grinning as HE turns to her on the way to the door.*) The end of the session. 'Bye, doc—(*HE opens the door and leaves.*)
SMYTHE. (*Stands, alarmed, shocked.*) Wait! Come back! Don't go ...

(*But HE has disappeared and SHE is left holding her pen, looking blankly at the door as the CURTAIN FALLS.*)

Scene 2

The same, a few months later.
JULIA SMYTHE is dictating into a machine. SHE wears different clothes, but the same crisp, no-nonsense style. SHE has half a dozen similar outfits at home and wears them throughout the week in a rota system. It's Thursday so it must be grey flannel.

SMYTHE. (*Into microphone.*) She no longer tries to deny her feelings towards her sister but instead attempts to place the cause of the neurosis upon inadequate paternal attention when she was a child.

(*Her intercom BUZZER sounds on the desk. SMYTHE flicks off the recorder and presses the intercom.*)

SMYTHE. Yes, Sally? ... Mr. Who? (*SHE riffles through some papers on her desk and finds the one she is seeking. As she does SHE repeats under her breath:*)

Millinchip … Millinchip …(*Reads letter.*) Ah yes … yes
… mmhmm …(*Presses intercom.*) Thank you, show him
in …

(*A moment later the door opens and a MAN in a raincoat
     enters. The collar is turned up and HE wears a trilby
     hat. Not much of his face can be seen.*)

SMYTHE. (*Stands and comes across, her hand firmly
outstretched.*) I won't be a second.

(*The MAN shuffles in, sticks out a hand and shakes hers.
     When SHE enters her routine manner, HE doesn't
     move. SHE turns, indicates a chair opposite her desk
     with a brief smile. SHE has turned her back on him to
     return to the chair behind the desk. The MAN takes off
     his hat and unbuttons his coat to reveal ADRIAN. HE
     has shorter hair now and lost the moustache. He wears
     an open neck shirt, casual jacket and trousers. It takes
     SMYTHE a few moments to sit down and pull across a
     folder containing some forms. ADRIAN stays by the
     door and waits for her to switch her attention from the
     folder to him. SHE looks up finally.*)

SMYTHE. Won't you sit down?

(*Surprised she doesn't recognize him, ADRIAN crosses the
     room and sits. SMYTHE takes her pen and a sheet from
     the folder.*)

SMYTHE. If we can get the formalities out of the way—(*SHE takes off her wrist watch and props it up on the desk top, then holds the pen hovering over the paper.*) May I have your full name?

ADRIAN. Adrian Wainwright.

SMYTHE. (*Writing.*) Adrian ... Wainwright ... Millinchip ...

ADRIAN. No. Just Adrian Wainwright.

SMYTHE. (*Frowns and picks up a letter.*) But your letter is signed A. Millinchip ...

ADRIAN. I lied.

SMYTHE. You lied about your *name*—?

ADRIAN. That's one of the reasons I'm here.

SMYTHE. (*Puts down the pen and clasps her hands together.*) You have a problem with your identity?

ADRIAN. Yes.

SMYTHE. (*Picks up the pen again.*) Adrian ... Wainwright ... address?

ADRIAN. Buckingham Palace, London S.W.1

SMYTHE. (*Starts to write, then looks at him sharply.*) Now look—

ADRIAN. I live in Chelsea. Just off the King's Road. I live with my mother and father and one sister ...

SMYTHE. (*Remembers. SHE puts down the pen again.*) Ah. Yes. I remember.

ADRIAN. I used a phoney name in the letter because I didn't think you would want to see me again.

SMYTHE. You are correct in your assumption.

ADRIAN. I came to apologize.

SMYTHE. It took you two months to pluck up the courage, I suppose.

ADRIAN. I had thought of writing to you. But in the end I realized these things have to be done face to face.

(SMYTHE sits back, takes a packet of cigarettes from a drawer and lights one.)

ADRIAN. You didn't used to smoke.
SMYTHE. Tell me about this—apology.
ADRIAN. What is there to tell? I'm sorry.
SMYTHE. Sorry for what?
ADRIAN. For winding you up.
SMYTHE. Oh, I see. That's what you were doing.
ADRIAN. Yes. And now I'm asking you to forgive me.
SMYTHE. *(Picking up her pen again, screwing on the top.)* There's really no need. I cannot believe that you give a damn if I forgive you or not.
ADRIAN. Actually, I didn't come back *only* to apologize.
SMYTHE. *(Puts the form in a waste basket.)* Well, whatever it is, be brief—

(SHE pretends to look at some other papers. ADRIAN doesn't move.)

ADRIAN. I came back because you wanted me to.'
SMYTHE. What do you mean?
ADRIAN. As I left, you were saying "Please don't go, come back ..."
SMYTHE. *(Gives him a firm and severe look. Had she been wearing glasses, she would have shot the expression over the top of them.)* I find that highly unlikely—

(HE puts a hand in his pocket and takes out a miniature tape recorder. HE plays it back a few seconds.)

SMYTHE. What are you doing—?

(HE presses the "play" switch and Smythe's voice is clearly heard along with his.)

ADRIAN'S VOICE. "... hold it to my mouth. My lips gently curl over—over the end and—oh, my God—"
SMYTHE. *(Standing, angry.)* You—you *recorded* us—!

(The RECORDER emits the pinging sound of the wrist watch alarm and of it being switched off with a thump. A pause.)

ADRIAN'S VOICE. "I made it ..."
SMYTHE'S VOICE. "You made what?"
SMYTHE. Get out of here—

(SHE goes to snatch the recorder but ADRIAN holds it out of her reach.)

ADRIAN'S VOICE. "The end of the session ...'Bye, doc ..."

(Some scuffling is heard, then:)

SMYTHE'S VOICE. "Wait! Come back! Don't go ..."

ADRIAN. (*Switches off the machine and looks at her.*)
Well—here I am.

SMYTHE. (*Glares at him and there is a physical effort
to remain calm involved. Finally SHE lowers her hands,
tries to relax her neck muscles and sits down again.*) I lied.

ADRIAN. No. That was what Mills and Boon would
call "a cry of anguish—" (*HE goes to play the last words
back again but SHE stops him.*)

SMYTHE. Please stop playing that thing!

ADRIAN. (*Puts it back in his pocket.*) You *do*
remember saying it—?

SMYTHE. Yes.

ADRIAN. What would have happened if I had come
back?

SMYTHE. I would probably have thrown this chair at
you.

ADRIAN. "I find that highly unlikely."

SMYTHE. (*Standing.*) I may well do it now, if you
don't leave this office.

ADRIAN. Frankly, I expected a rather more mature
reaction.

SMYTHE. You come here, you waste my time,
inventing some stories that I have no reason to disbelieve.
Then you tell me the whole thing was some feeble joke at
my expense. And now you say you expected a more mature
reaction? You're not just a fool. You're an arrogant fool.

ADRIAN. (*Remains smiling and when she finishes taps
the recorder.*) You knew it was a joke when I walked out.
Why did you want me to come back?

SMYTHE. (*Sits down again.*) I didn't feel we had
finished.

ADRIAN. Your alarm went off—

SMYTHE. I'm not governed by an alarm—

ADRIAN. No? Then why did you insist that I stayed until the end of the session?

SMYTHE. (*He has a point and SHE shows it my a slight fidget of her feet.*) I suppose I was curious to know why anyone would play such a mindless stunt.

ADRIAN. Yet now, a couple of months on, you don't give a damn.

SMYTHE. I had forgotten about you. I had assumed you were nothing more than a spoiled brat with time on his hands who took delight in playing childish games.

ADRIAN. Is that what you think now?

SMYTHE. Yes.

ADRIAN. You have no interest at all in knowing why I wound you up—?

SMYTHE. You are obviously dying to tell me.

ADRIAN. I wanted to find out just how gullible you were.

SMYTHE. (*Lights another cigarette, sits back and glares at him.*) Gullible—

ADRIAN. Yes.

SMYTHE. And you found out.

ADRIAN. Yes.

SMYTHE. And I suppose it made you feel good.

ADRIAN. I felt justified.

SMYTHE. *Justified?* About what?

ADRIAN. About thinking that your profession is nothing more than a cynical way to make money. A cruel trick played upon the weak and the insecure.

SMYTHE. (*Manages a humorless laugh, a slight baring of the teeth.*) Ah. That old one.

ADRIAN. Everyone loves to talk about themselves. It's everyone's favorite topic. You and your kind pulled off an amazing coup. You actually got people to *pay* to do it. It's like getting them to pay you to *breathe*! All you do is sit here and pretend to listen. On your own admission, you don't *cure* them of anything. In fact, as I proved, you discourage any idea that *that* is what you're here to do.

SMYTHE. You *proved* it—?

ADRIAN. You suggested that my mother was the reason for my impotence. I said you were absolutely right and that I felt my sexual powers returning almost at once. I wanted to pay up and leave right then. Remember what your reaction was—? (*HE half brings out the recorder.*)

SMYTHE. I remember—

ADRIAN. You were horrified! *Leave* after ten minutes thinking you were *cured*—? How preposterous! So you went banging on about sexual intimidation, being a closet homosexual, about *smell*. You cleared the pool in double quick time, then you took a stick and stirred up the mud again to avoid making me believe I was cured. Telling me you weren't a garage, your job wasn't to produce snap *results*. No, it isn't. Your job is to make sure the punters come back next week and pay another fifty quid.

(*A long silence. SMYTHE takes some sharp drags on the cigarette, avoiding ADRIAN's stare.*)

ADRIAN. There's a smugness built into your work that's designed to make you leave this office at night feeling good. "All these whackos! All these weird problems people have! Thank God I'm normal." Doctor, you say you are here for the sake of your clients. It's the other way round. The poor sods who trip in here every day only serve to keep you sane.

(Another lengthy pause.)

SMYTHE. Am I to understand you were telling lies from the moment you came in here?
ADRIAN. Before, actually.
SMYTHE. *(SHE glances at him again.)* Before—?
ADRIAN. My real name isn't Adrian Wainwright.
SMYTHE. Really.
ADRIAN. But it'll do for now.
SMYTHE. You father doesn't work for M.I. 6?
ADRIAN. He's an accountant.
SMYTHE. The depressed mother, the impotence, the demanding girl friend—
ADRIAN. It was true about the figs. I've always found them sexy.
SMYTHE. And you went to all this trouble, you invented all these stories—merely to show that my profession is a fraud?
ADRIAN. Yes.

(A long pause as SMYTHE pulls on her cigarette and aims a plume of smoke at the ceiling.)

SMYTHE. What a pathetic little fucker you are.

ADRIAN. (*Surprised at her calm but direct response, makes a small grin of semi embarrassment.*) I resent the "pathetic" and the "little." "Fucker" yes. I never was impotent.

SMYTHE. (*Picks up the tape on the desk and drops it again.*) I wouldn't be surprised if you were taping this as well.

(*ADRIAN pauses, then puts his hand in his pocket and with a smile puts a second machine on the desk. It is turning. SMYTHE doesn't touch it. SHE taps her fingers a moment, then stubs out the cigarette.*)

SMYTHE. My guess would be, you're a tabloid journalist—or a student working on a piece called something like: "Up Yours, Mr. Freud." My money's on the hack.

ADRIAN. I'm not working for anyone or anything.

SMYTHE. Then why bother?

ADRIAN. To prove my point.

SMYTHE. You haven't proved anything. You had a point of view before you came here and all you've done is select a few things to reinforce it. You have the mind of a bigot.

ADRIAN. You could have *dis*proved it.

SMYTHE. How?

ADRIAN. I've told you. When I said I thought I was cured, when I asked to leave to put it to the test, you should have said "Good idea, I hope it works, that'll be fifty pounds, bye bye."

SMYTHE. (*Pauses, knowing this is a weak part of her argument.*) That isn't the way psychiatry operates.

ADRIAN. When I have a sore throat, the doctor prescribes some medicine. He says if it doesn't work, come back and try something else. Why can't you do that?

SMYTHE. Medical diagnosis is much simpler than psychiatric. Your sore throat is visible. Someone comes in here with a mental block of some sort, it doesn't show.

ADRIAN. (*Smiling.*) Wrong. The answer is, the doctor's a G.P. He doesn't get paid. It's in, out and onto the next.

SMYTHE. You've made up your mind that we're only here for the money.

ADRIAN. Still haven't answered the big one, doc. Why didn't you let me go after I said I was cured?

SMYTHE. I didn't believe you were.

ADRIAN. Why didn't you let me run a test?

SMYTHE. As you told it, your case was interesting.

ADRIAN. You mean it had everything? Mother love, espionage, nymphomania, a hint of homosexuality. I tried to include everything. Maybe I could have arrived in a dress.

SMYTHE. I wanted you to stay because I was intrigued.

ADRIAN. Curing the patient is secondary to stimulating your interest, is that it?

SMYTHE. I don't cure.

ADRIAN. Male impotence fascinates women, doesn't it?

ADRIAN. I can't speak for all women.

ADRIAN. For you, then.

SMYTHE. Fascination is hardly the word.

ADRIAN. What *is* the word?

SMYTHE. It's of interest, certainly.

ADRIAN. Because if you take sexual power away from a man, he no longer fits the stereotype. Didn't one of the sisterhood once say that all men were rapists?

SMYTHE. They might have. Stupidity is not the prerogative of my sex.

ADRIAN. An impotent man is not your image of a male human being.

SMYTHE. Nonsense. That is like saying a woman who cannot conceive does not regard herself as female.

ADRIAN. Infertile women say it all the time. Well, those who discuss themselves in newspapers do.

SMYTHE. They are wrong.

ADRIAN. Why? Because you say so?

SMYTHE. If you like. If they think that, then it is the job of psychiatry to change their minds.

ADRIAN. Have you ever had a woman come to you and say they do not feel a whole person because they cannot bear children?

SMYTHE. Yes.

ADRIAN. And did you cure them—?

SMYTHE/ADRIAN. (*Together.*) "I don't cure—"

ADRIAN. I know.

SMYTHE. I think I helped them come to terms with themselves.

ADRIAN. You *think*?

SMYTHE. They stopped coming after a while.

ADRIAN. If I go to a laundry and they keep on wrecking my clothes, I stop going too. What I do is, I find another laundry.

SMYTHE. True, they may well have found another analyst. I don't claim a hundred percent success rate.

ADRIAN. You don't claim *any* success rate. No cure, no success.

SMYTHE. Your definition. Not mine.

(A pause.)

SMYTHE. When you spoke of loving the cinema—"with a passion," I think you said—was that a lie as well?

ADRIAN. Yes.

SMYTHE. I can understand you making up a bizarre sexual problem for me to trip over, but to lie about something as trivial as the cinema ...

(ADRIAN starts to wander round the room, smiling. HE is in the driver's seat. HE feels confident. HE is teaching her about things she seems to know nothing about.)

ADRIAN. Let me explain about improvising.

SMYTHE. About lying, you mean—

ADRIAN. Just shut up a minute. When I was here before, you said that I would talk and you would listen. Where was I?

(SHE remains silent.)

ADRIAN. Improvising is a matter of building on whatever the other person says. You asked me if I liked the cinema. I said yes. Actually I hardly ever go.

SMYTHE. You could have said no.

ADRIAN. Improvising is a matter of keep talking. Where do you go from no? End of conversation.

(A pause.)

SMYTHE. Finished?

(HE grins and nods.)

SMYTHE. You call that improvising. I call it lying.

ADRIAN. All right—

SMYTHE. And your tragedy is you don't know the difference.

ADRIAN. Tragedy? For someone so precise on the meaning of words, doctor, isn't that a little strong?

SMYTHE. Not at all. For instance, you are abroad. It's pouring with rain. I telephone you and ask what the weather's like. You'd explain in the most lyrical terms how it's a hundred in the shade and the birds are dropping from the trees. If it were sunny, you'd give a poetic account of a monsoon. Correct?

ADRIAN. *(Doesn't answer at once and a nervous smile betrays she is right.)* Perhaps.

SMYTHE. Why? Why would you do that?

ADRIAN. I guess lying is easier than telling the truth.

SMYTHE. And why do you think that is?

ADRIAN. (*Uncertain.*) I suppose ... I really don't know.

SMYTHE. You don't tell the truth because you are unable to describe what you actually *see* or what you really *think*. For instance—describe this desk.

ADRIAN. The desk?

SMYTHE. Anything that comes into your head.

ADRIAN. (*Hesitates, then shrugs, then tries.*) It's ... er ... made of wood ... got some drawers on either side ... leather top. Maybe old, could be a reproduction ... (*HE ends with a shrug.*)

SMYTHE. You really made that come alive.

ADRIAN. What else is there to say about a bloody desk?

SMYTHE. This classic piece of craftsmanship dates from 1778. It has survived countless moves over two hundred years. How many famous elbows have rested on the top? How many wise or foolish, kind or cruel words have been spoken across it? Perhaps Jane Austen wrote "Pride and Prejudice" here. Darwin his "Origin of Species." Or maybe Jack the Ripper conceived his bloody mania in that chair? Was it there that Haig planned the battles of the First War that wiped out a generation? Did Churchill's fingers grasp the edge when he heard about Dunkirk? How many secrets have been absorbed in its mellow surface? How many tears of grief have fallen on its grain? We shall never know. (*A pause.*) You might have said something like that.

(ADRIAN stands still for several moments. SMYTHE looks at him without expression, increasing his sense of unease.)

SMYTHE. Except, of course, you wouldn't have. You'd have said Jane Austen *did* write here, Jack the Ripper *did* own it, Churchill *did* use it. I can use my imagination without lying. You can't. And that's the tragedy.

(HE has nothing to say. HE squirms, uncomfortable beneath HER steady gaze, and avoids her eyes. SHE comes closer and almost compels HIM to look at her.)

SMYTHE. Lies only affect the person telling them. When you tell me your father works for the Secret Service, I'm not impressed. But you are. And soon you come to believe it. Soon you find you've woven a fantasy world around yourself. And soon you find you're unable to escape from it, and soon you go mad.
  ADRIAN. And soon I kill myself?
  SMYTHE. No. Soon you come to people like me.

(There follows a long silence. ADRIAN sits down slowly and stares at her. SHE holds his gaze.)

ADRIAN. You think I'm mad?
SMYTHE. As the proverbial hatter.
ADRIAN. And I only came here for help.
SMYTHE. You're begging for it. Every fibre of your being is in panic. Your grasp on reality is slipping by the day. You can't even remember your real name. Soon you

will come to believe that you *are* impotent, that your father *is* a spy. That your mother *is* depressed when you aren't at home. Your fingers will scrabble to regain a hold but inch by inch they will slide away from the ledge. Who was Anna? Did she really exist? Did we *really* make love in the cinema? Did I once like to eat figs—or was it bananas? Did I once dream that I went to a psychiatrist? Did she tell me my mother was to blame for something? Or did I really go? And why? And then your mind dissolves, like burning paper and you fall into that dark abyss where all thought is drowned by the sound of one eternal primal scream.

(*NEITHER of them move for a long moment. Then ADRIAN's head droops. HE closes his eyes and starts to weep silently.*
SMYTHE watches him. SHE stays seated, her hands clasped together, elbows resting lightly on the desk.
The ALARM on her watch goes off. SHE lets it sound for some seconds before shutting it off. As she does, HER face breaks into a wide smile.)

SMYTHE. Made it.

(*ADRIAN looks up, his eyes moist, an expression of bewilderment on his face.*)

ADRIAN. (*Hoarsely.*) What? ... made what?
SMYTHE. The end of the session. (*SHE stands, replaces the watch on her wrist and clears up the folders on the desk matter of factly.*) Goodbye.

*(But ADRIAN doesn't move. HE looks at her blankly.
SHE goes to the door, opens it and waits, smiling
broadly. Then SHE goes out.)*

ADRIAN. Wait. Don't go ... Come back ...!

(The CURTAIN FALLS.)

ACT I

Scene 3

*The same. A few days later.
SMYTHE enters in a smart topcoat as her TELEPHONE
is ringing. SHE picks it up.*

SMYTHE. Hello, Julia Smythe. *(As she listens, SHE
pulls a face. SHE sits back, pushing her chair a foot or so
from the desk. When SHE speaks it is that mechanical way
used for callers who are well known but not welcome.)*
Hello, Charles ... I'm fine, how are you? ... No, not
really, it's only been three months ... How long is Barbara
away this time? ... I know, Charles, because I know you
... All right, just tell me if I get anything wrong. Ready?
Barbara left two days ago. You spent the first night alone
doing all the things you can't when your wife is there. You
hired a couple of pornographic videos, smoked a cigar,
snacked on a little caviar and knocked off a bottle of your
best claret. How am I doing? Then as your mind became

filled with the bums and the tits and the booze, your romantic nature made you think back over our ten golden years together! No, Charles, let me finish, you'll get your turn. You tried to forget me but damn it if there wasn't a few embers still flickering. So when you got to the office this morning, you called to find out if there was fuck on for tonight ... Did I get anything wrong? ... Ah, Barbara left three days ago, not two ... your self-control is an inspiration to us all ... What makes you think I'm upset? You decided ten years was long enough to have what's known as a bit on the side. It might have been nice had you come out and said so, instead of merely lengthening the times between your phone calls ... (*Listens a long time, speaks mechanically.*) Oh, how sweet ... Nooooo, my dear, I don't think so. One never crosses the same river twice ... A lot has changed ... Weeeeeell, it pains me to say this but you're not getting any younger ... sex *is* important, Charles ... no, companionship *doesn't* come into it. When you decided not to ask Barbara for a divorce all those years ago, you made it clear to me that companionship was to be found at home, not with me. (*SHE listens for about ten seconds.*) All right, Charles, I'll have dinner with you tonight ... Yes, yes I can't wait to hear all about the hunting ... And your children ... James still in America, is he? And what about your daughters still being expelled from school ...? (*Her INTERCOM buzzers.*) Hang on—(*Presses the button.*) Yes, Sally? ... Er—all right, I'll take it— (*To Charles.*) Charles, hold on a minute—I've got an urgent call on the other line. (*Presses a phone button.*) Hello ... Yes, it is ... (*SHE listens and becomes alarmed, alert.*) When did this happen? ... (*Picks up a pen.*) What's the address ...? (*As SHE writes quickly.*) Have you called an ambulance...? I see. One question— how did you get my name? ... Yes, I'll be there in twenty minutes. (*SHE ends the call. SHE stands shocked, stuck to the floor, devastated by what she has heard. SHE brings up a hand and wipes her face, lost in a fog of tumbling random thoughts for several moments. Finally SHE presses the telephone button.*) Charles? I can't see you tonight—(*SHE puts down the receiver at once. Then SHE hurries to the door, grabbing her coat and shoulder bag, and rushes out.*)

(*The CURTAIN FALLS.*)

ACT I

Scene 4

A bed sitting room, perhaps in the Earls Court area, where rooms have been converted years ago to accommodate the footloose, transient youth of several generations.

Somewhere at the back is a space in the corner converted into a tiny cooking area with a sink, a cupboard and an immersion heater. A window looks out onto other Victorian buildings.

The main entrance door is half off its hinges and there is a split beside the lock.

A set of cheap shelves contain a row of paperbacks, a hi-fi and a TV.

*The main feature of the room is a single bed. In it, propped
up on pillows and looking pretty awful, lies ADRIAN.
A side table holds a lamp and next to it is a wardrobe.
The only other piece of furniture in the room is a worn
armchair. A telephone is near the bed.*

*ADRIAN doesn't move. The only sign he is conscious is
that his eyes are open, but they remain fixed on some
invisible point halfway across the room. As the curtain
rises FOOTSTEPS can be heard mounting stairs.*

*A SCUFFLE grows louder outside and someone pushes
open the door, scraping the bottom edge across the floor
as the one hinge in place lets it swing unsteadily back.*

*SMYTHE comes in. She has come straight from her
office. In one hand is an opened envelope and letter.*

*SHE enters cautiously, looking at the broken door before
coming slowly across to stand beside the bed.*

*So far, ADRIAN has made no sign that he is aware anyone
has come in.*

SMYTHE. Hello ... (*No response.*) How are you?

ADRIAN. (*Moves his head an inch. HE glances at her a
moment. A mumble.*) Never felt better. Love a game of
squash. It's really good to see you. (*A long pause.*) As you
see, I'm still a compulsive liar.

SMYTHE. Is there anything I can get for you?

ADRIAN. You don't happen to have a sugar-coated
cyanide pill—?

SMYTHE. (*Takes off her coat and places the bag on the
carpet.*) You look awful.

ADRIAN. I'm sorry. If I'd known you were coming, I'd
have had a wash.

SMYTHE. I gather you owe your life to the man
downstairs.

ADRIAN. Yes. Sod him.

SMYTHE. Lucky he knew what do do.

ADRIAN. You don't need seven years of medical school
to stick a couple of nicotined fingers down somebody's
throat.

SMYTHE. How many pills did you take?

ADRIAN. Not enough apparently.

SMYTHE. I think you should be in the hospital.

ADRIAN. I think you should go away.

SMYTHE. You need proper supervision and treatment.

ADRIAN. Look, why did you come here?

SMYTHE. (*Holds up the letter in her hand.*) Your friend
downstairs opened the note you left.

ADRIAN. That dago bastard—

SMYTHE. Since you didn't address it to anyone—
(*Shows a blank envelope.*)—he had every right to.

ADRIAN. He had no right to give it to you—

SMYTHE. (*SHE takes the letter out.*) Can you
remember what you wrote?

ADRIAN. Some ...

SMYTHE. (*Opens it up.*) Did you mean what you said?

ADRIAN. Suicide notes *tend* to be written with
sincerity.

SMYTHE. (*Starts to read.*) "To whom it may
concern—" (*Looks at him.*) Suicide notes *don't* tend to
start like that—

ADRIAN. You've read a few in your time, have you?
Clients, no doubt.

SMYTHE. (*Reading.*) "I am taking my life because it has been made clear to me that I am insane—unable to distinguish between fact and fantasy. As Doctor Julia Smythe, a well-known psychiatrist and expert in her field, so succinctly put it, I am as mad as the proverbial hatter—" (*Stops.*) Why did you write that?

ADRIAN. Because you said it. I've got it on tape—

SMYTHE. I *meant*, why did you describe me as "Well-known" and "an expert in my field"?

ADRIAN. *Aren't* you?

SMYTHE. I am certainly not well-known, and you certainly do not regard me as an expert. I want to know why you wrote it.

ADRIAN. "The balance of my mind was disturbed"—

SMYTHE. (*Glares at him and continues to read.*) "I did not want to believe this, and tried hard to convince myself that she didn't know what she was talking about. She is, after all, a sexually frustrated, middle-aged and lonely woman who might resent a younger man doubting her motives as a psychiatrist—"

ADRIAN. I'm sorry—

SMYTHE. (*Continues to read after a moment.*) "But I thought over what she had said and later, in the silence of my room, I realized she was right. I have wondered for some time about my mental state. And now Doctor Smythe has confirmed all my worst fears. She has told me that shortly I would cease to have a grasp on reality and that I would fall into everlasting torment. Rather than wait for that moment, I have decided to end my life now. To my parents, my friends, to God, I say 'forgive me.' Goodbye."

(*SMYTHE lays the letter down on the bed. It stays on the blankets untouched by either of them.*)

ADRIAN. Look, I'm sorry I said you were sexually frustrated and—

SMYTHE. That's quite irrelevant. What I'm unable to understand is that you tried to kill yourself because of what I said.

ADRIAN. You didn't give me any hope. All that stuff about abysses and primal screams—

SMYTHE. I didn't *mean* it! Do you seriously think I go around calling clients mad as a hatter? That I terrify them with visions of hell? *Do* you?

ADRIAN. But ... you did, you ...

SMYTHE. Look—I wanted *you* to know how it felt to listen to someone, believe them—only to be told the whole thing was a joke! What you did to me was so—so humiliating! When you walked out, *laughing*, it was like—like rape! I felt violated. Degraded. For a long while afterwards, all I could think about was getting even with you. Then, suddenly, there you were. I realized—here was my chance! God knows why I did, I must have been completely out of control, but the longer you went on the more I thought to myself, if only I can keep him here until my alarm goes off! I could do *exactly* what he did to me. And it worked! The symmetry was perfect. (*A pause, SHE comes down, hold up the letter.*) Until I read this! (*SHE lets it drop onto the bed. Long pause.*)

ADRIAN. I really did come to you for help. I've always known I was a fantasist. It started when I was a child and just sort of—grew. I wanted help, but I couldn't just come to you and say: "Doctor, I have this weird problem, please do something—" I still had to invent things. All that stuff about my parents, and impotence. I was so ashamed of myself when I got home and remembered what I'd done, it took me two months to pluck up enough courage to face you again. And when I did—I *still* couldn't tell you straight! I *still* couldn't tell the plain truth! I still had to lie! Play those bloody tapes! (*HE stops and there is a pause as HE wipes his eyes on the bedsheets.*) But you got through in the end. It was when you said improvising was just another word for lying. I knew I was getting close to coming out with everything. When—when you said I was mad—you only confirmed what I already thought ... (*HE sighs, long and painfully.*) When you left the room, I didn't blame you. You had every right. I didn't blame you at all. It was no more than I deserved.

(*SMYTHE reaches into her bag and finds cigarettes. SHE lights one and draws deeply. SHE watches HIM wince as HE changes positions in bed.*)

SMYTHE. You really ought to see a doctor.
ADRIAN. I'll be O.K. My ribs are just sore from all the throwing up. I'm thirsty—

(*SHE fetches a drink of water and HE gulps it down. As he does, SHE looks at the broken door.*)

SMYTHE. The man below—
ADRIAN. Carlos—
SMYTHE. Did he do that?
ADRIAN. What?

SMYTHE. (*Pointing.*) The door.

ADRIAN. Yes.

SMYTHE. How did he know something was wrong?

ADRIAN. (*Points to the hi-fi and CD equipment.*) Mozart saved my life.

SMYTHE. Mozart?

ADRIAN. After I took the pills, I had this wild idea that I wanted to go out listening to Mozart's *Requiem* playing full blast. Apparently the CD stuck. Carlos heard it and knocked on the door. When he got no answer, he broke in and found me out for the count. Saw the pill bottle and guessed the rest.

SMYTHE. Why didn't he call an ambulance?

ADRIAN. This place is full of illegal immigrants. From Colombia mostly. He was scared to phone the police.

SMYTHE. Thank God he had the sense to find me in the telephone book.

ADRIAN. That, I could have done without.

SMYTHE. I'm talking about the letter—(*SHE points to it.*) If anyone else had read that, I'd have been ruined.

ADRIAN. Why?

SMYTHE. (*Manages a thin smile.*) Believe me, when clients try and kill themselves because their analyst has told them they are barking mad, it doesn't look very good.

ADRIAN. I'm sorry.

SMYTHE. I wish you'd stop apologizing.

ADRIAN. I meant the letter to show that you'd been right and I'd been wrong.

(*A pause.*)

SMYTHE. Carlos called you Adrian.
ADRIAN. Yes ...?
SMYTHE. So it *is* your real name after all.
ADRIAN. (*Shrugs and bares his teeth in a weak smile.*)
I'm afraid so. Adrian Wainwright.
SMYTHE. Do I believe you this time or not?
ADRIAN. Please yourself.

(*SHE has calmed down now and is trying to lower the awkward tenseness between them.*)

ADRIAN. Would you like some coffee?
SMYTHE. All right.

(*HE pulls aside the blankets to stand up.*)

SMYTHE. I'll make it—
ADRIAN. (*Sharply.*) No! (*Softer.*) I'm O.K. Let me do
it. Please—

(*SHE stops and shrugs. SHE watches HIM have a bit of a tussle pulling aside the blankets and sheets, disentangling himself from the mess of bedclothes. When HE stands and moves upstage to the kitchen area, SHE is alarmed to see HE is nude. SHE turns away. Unaware of her reaction, ADRIAN reaches the sink and fills a kettle. As he does so HE looks over his shoulder.*)

ADRIAN. Don't you have any clients this morning?

SMYTHE. Not until eleven—

(*HE notices she doesn't turn around. When the kettle is filled HE looks down at himself and realizes why she is being so discreet.*)

ADRIAN. Oh, Jesus Christ, I'm sorry! (*HE snatches at a towel beside the sink and holds it round his waist as HE returns to the bed.*) I didn't realize—I'm still a bit dopey—
SMYTHE. It's perfectly all right—

(*By now ADRIAN has reached a dressing gown lying on the floor by the bed and put it on. HE goes back to the kitchen area and plugs in the kettle, finds the instant coffee and the mugs. As he does HE sees SMYTHE looking over the room.*)

ADRIAN. (*Imitating Bette Davis.*) "What a dump!"
SMYTHE. (*Turns now and looks questioningly at him.*) What?
ADRIAN. In the worst film Bette Davis ever made, a real turkey called *Beyond the Forest* she comes into a house and says: "What a dump!" Every time you mention her name to a film buff, they'll probably say: "What a dump!"
SMYTHE. Of course. You once ran a season of the world's worst movies, I recall.
ADRIAN. Odd how she's remembered for a line from her lousiest picture.
SMYTHE. You told me the cinema was your passion. Then you said it didn't interest you at all. Which is it?
ADRIAN. The first was true. The second is a lie.

SMYTHE. So you *do* like films—

ADRIAN. My favorite line from Bette Davis is in *Whatever Happened to Baby Jane?* When her crippled sister, played by Joan Crawford, says to her: "You wouldn't talk to me like this if I weren't in this wheelchair." Davis says: "But you *are*, Blanche. You *are!*" That has to be the cruelest line ever written.

SMYTHE. And yet you say it's your favorite.

ADRIAN. Yes. All great humor is rooted in cruelty. Don't you think?

(The kettle is WHISTLING and ADRIAN goes through the ritual of pouring the two mugs of coffee as they speak. SMYTHE is glancing at the paperback books on the shelf.)

SMYTHE. I don't know about cruelty—

(ADRIAN brings the coffees across. HE walks slowly, stiffly but SMYTHE makes no attempt to meet him halfway—assuming he doesn't want that. SHE takes the mug HE offers, remains standing while HE lowers himself cautiously to sit on the bed.)

ADRIAN. Maybe cruelty is the wrong word. All humor is rooted in pain. I think that's what I believe.

SMYTHE. You may be right.

(THEY sip the coffee in silence.
SHE looks around the room. There is a small portable television.)

SMYTHE. Where are all of your videos?

ADRIAN. What videos?

SMYTHE. At the same time that you told me you were mad about the cinema—which is now true, isn't it?

ADRIAN. Yes—

SMYTHE. You also said you had taped hundred of films off television.

ADRIAN. (*Pauses, grins.*) That bit was *not* true.

(*HE smiles and SMYTHE nods. A silence continues as THEY sip the coffee.*)

SMYTHE. How do I know you're not lying now?

ADRIAN. You don't.

SMYTHE. This conversation we're having—your part of it could be pure fantasy.

ADRIAN. Yes.

SMYTHE. You say you like the cinema, then you say you don't, then you say you do. Truth—lie—truth. Right?

ADRIAN. Yes.

SMYTHE. Equally it could be lie—truth—lie.

ADRIAN. Yes, it could.

SMYTHE. After all, you're not cured of your addiction to making things up, are you?

ADRIAN. No. But you have to admit, I do know quite a bit about the movies.

SMYTHE. Quotations—

ADRIAN. Yes. And what films they are from. I bet if you ask anyone who goes to the pictures about Bette Davis they still won't have heard of *Beyond the Forest.*

SMYTHE. (*Puts down her cup and crosses to the bookshelf. SHE takes a book down and holds it for him to see.*) *Famous Quotations from the Movies.*

ADRIAN. (*Pauses, smiles self-consciously.*) My, my. What big eyes you have Grandma ...

SMYTHE. (*Opens it at the back and runs a finger down an index.*) "Bette Davis ... page one hundred and twelve ..."

ADRIAN. I haven't looked at that book in years—

SMYTHE. (*Flips to the front.*) First published last December —

ADRIAN. (*Begins to sound edgy.*) Why are you suddenly being so hostile—?

SMYTHE. (*Finds the page and reads.*) "What a dump!" Said on entering a room, *Beyond the Forest,* 1949.

"But you are, Blanche, you are"—to Joan Crawford, her crippled sister, when told she would not talk to her so rudely if she were not in a wheelchair. *Whatever Happened to Baby Jane?*, 1962.

"Oh Jerry, why ask for the moon? We have the stars." Final lines of *Now Voyager.*

ADRIAN. Look, what's the point of this?

SMYTHE. (*Closes the book and puts it back on the shelf.*) I'll tell you the point. The point is this. As far as I'm concerned, you're blown. The jig is up. Whether you tell me the truth or tell me lies, it makes no difference. I'm not going to believe *anything* you say. Not one word. What's the time?

ADRIAN. (*Looks at his watch.*) Half past ten.

SMYTHE. (*Makes quite a slow, deliberate show of baring her wrist, holding an arm up in front of her face and studying her own watch.*) Yes. So it is. You're right. (*SHE*

lowers the arm and looks across at him.) Tell me
something else.

ADRIAN. *(Thinks, looks at the window.)* It's a nice
day.

SMYTHE. *(Walks slowly, deliberately to the window,
throws up the sash and looks out, leaning quite far and
craning her neck. SHE pulls herself back in, closing the
window.)* No, it's not.

ADRIAN. I can see the sun—

SMYTHE. Liar. It's pouring with rain.

ADRIAN. *(Stands and stumbles across, lifts the
window.)* It's a lovely day!

SMYTHE. *(Returns to her coffee and picks up the mug,
sips.)* You're wrong. You're suffering from delusions. It's
wet and miserable out there.

ADRIAN. *(Looks back at her, grins and shuts the
window, returns, folding the lapels of his dressing gown
into each other, as if cold.)* You're right, I'm sorry.

SMYTHE. Right about what?

ADRIAN. The rain.

SMYTHE. *(Going to the window.)* What rain? The sun
is shining.

ADRIAN. *(Sits, then lies on the bed, looking tired.)*
Can we play something else now, doctor?

SMYTHE. Is Carlos a friend of yours?

ADRIAN. Not really.

SMYTHE. Do you have any friends?

ADRIAN. Tons.

SMYTHE. Do you lie to them?

ADRIAN. Yes. I told you. I can't help myself.

SMYTHE. If you have tons of friends, how is it you couldn't think of one to address your suicide note to?

ADRIAN. (*HE buries his head in the pillow.*) I'm tired. Why don't you go away? (*HE hauls the blankets over him.*)

(*SMYTHE finishes her coffee, goes to the sink and puts the cup under the tap, washes it up, then dries it. When he hears the water run, ADRIAN looks across at her and watches her clean and dry the cup.*)

ADRIAN. You're very anal, aren't you?

SMYTHE. (*Looks back and smiles.*) Don't use words you don't understand.

ADRIAN. I do understand "anal." They use it in your business.

SMYTHE. (*Now SHE is cleaning the sink.*) What do you think it means?

ADRIAN. It means being too precise. You're doing it now. You clean the cups, then the saucers, then the spoons—Christ now you're even cleaning the sink.

SMYTHE. Too precise, you say—

ADRIAN. Everything has to be symmetrical. Like in your office. You had to do exactly what I did—wait until your alarm went off and walk out, making me say what you said: "Don't go, come back—"

SMYTHE. Symmetrical—

ADRIAN. Yes. Neat—

SMYTHE. (*Carefully arranging the two clean cups and the saucers on the kitchen ledge, taking her time about it. Then SHE turns and folds her arms.*) It means nothing of the sort. "Anal" means someone who likes sodomy. That's all.

ADRIAN. That's not true—!

(HE struggles to get off the bed and makes his way across to the bookshelf, holding on to the back of the armchair as he goes, the room a series of crutches for him to sustain his weak legs. HE looks along the books and finds one, pulls it off the shelf.)

ADRIAN. In here—*A Dictionary of Psychiatry*—

SMYTHE. Don't you ever read any proper books? Tolstoy ... or John Le Carré?

ADRIAN. *(Has now looked up the word.)* "Anal—a psychiatric term to indicate an excessive attention to neatness. Fastidious, ordered—" There!

SMYTHE. That's what I said.

ADRIAN. You didn't! You made some stupid joke about sodomy!

SMYTHE. *(Walks over to him with a slow measured pace and a smile to match. SHE takes the book from his hands and closes it, puts it back on the shelf.)* You're confused.

ADRIAN. You did!

(SHE is giving him a helping hand and HE limps across the floor holding onto her arm until SHE decants him back on the bed. As she goes, SHE says:)

SMYTHE. One of the after effects of an overdose is quite often hallucination—

ADRIAN. I know what you're doing, you're trying to make me believe I'm hearing things—well, it won't work, *doctor*!

(When THEY reach the bed SHE gives him quite a hard shove that makes him bounce slightly as he hits the mattress. Then SHE leans over him and HE recoils, scared.)

SMYTHE. How many fingers am I holding up? *(SHE raises four fingers.)*
ADRIAN. Four—
SMYTHE. *(Slaps him quite hard on the cheek.)* Wrong! How many now? *(SHE holds up one.)*
ADRIAN. One!
SMYTHE. *(Hits him again.)* You're lying—
ADRIAN. I'm not! I can see one finger—!

(But now SHE has changed to two fingers.)

ADRIAN. No, two—

(SHE hits him again, harder and HE covers his face. SHE backs off and stands, her arms folded.)

SMYTHE. This is going to take longer than I thought.
ADRIAN. Go away! I didn't want you to come here. Leave me alone ...
SMYTHE. I'm not going anywhere.
ADRIAN. You said you had a client at eleven—
SMYTHE. No, I didn't.

ADRIAN. (*Looking at his watch.*) It's almost eleven now—

SMYTHE. (*Looking at hers.*) No, it's not.

(*ADRIAN stuffs his face into his pillow and gives a muffled cry of pain.*)

SMYTHE. You're not going to get away with it as easily as that.

ADRIAN. (*Muffled in the pillow.*) Get away with what—?

SMYTHE. You made sure that if you were going to die, you'd ruin me. (*Picks up letter.*) You wrote that letter deliberately in such a way that a coroner's court would decide that I had *forced* you to commit suicide. But, as in everything else, you failed. You *didn't* die. I'm going to do something I've never done before.

ADRIAN. (*Lifts his head from the pillow.*) What?

(*SMYTHE comes to the side of his bed. HE cowers back against the headboard but she doesn't bend over him. SHE smiles brightly and puts on her coat, picking up her bag.*)

SMYTHE. I'm going to cure you.

(*ADRIAN stumbles out of bed and falls to the floor as SHE heads for the doorway.*)

ADRIAN. Leave me alone! I don't want you here! Go away! I don't want to see you again ... I—I hate you ...!

(SMYTHE turns and smiles brightly at him as HE crawls towards her on the floor. SHE raises her hand and flutters her fingers in a farewell gesture, then exits and as ADRIAN reaches the door painfully on his stomach, calling:)

ADRIAN. Stay away from me! I'll call the police! Do you hear me! Do you—hear—me—!

(HE cries out and rests his head exhaustedly on the ground. Her FOOTSTEPS recede down the uncarpeted steps, until he can no longer hear them.
Once there is silence, ADRIAN lifts his head up sharply. HE leaps to his feet and tiptoes to the doorway and looks out and downwards.
Then HE comes back into the room, raises his hands like a footballer who has just scored and does a sudden and energetic forward flip, landing neatly on his toes, knees bent.
HE goes to a telephone and dials. As he waits, HE takes out some ten pound notes from a drawer.)

ADRIAN. Carlos? Muchos gracias, amigo. I couldn't have done it without your help. I'll bring your money down—

(The CURTAIN FALLS.)

ACT II

Scene 1

Three months later.

*We are still in Adrian's flat, but it takes a few moments to
    realize the fact. Everything has changed except for the
    structural composition of the room. The window is now
    framed by a pair of tastefully colorful curtains. The door
    is now repaired and freshly painted, a new rug lies on
    the floor and the kitchen area is shiny and pin neat. On
    the bed is a bright duvet, matching the curtains, and the
    bedside tables are contemporary glass design. Even the
    telephone has been switched, a sleek new white set, the
    pride of British Telecom, has replaced the ancient black
    model of old.*

*The shelves have given way to a unit which neatly houses
    the hi-fi, TV, CDs and records along with many more
    books than before.*

*The new piece of furniture is a desk placed beneath the
    window with a "pew-style" seat, the kind designed to
    reduce back ache. A typewriter stands on the desk and
    some A4 paper is neatly stacked on one side.*

*The armchairs are new as well, as are the cooking pans
    hanging in a row of declining size beside the oven.*

*After a moment, ADRIAN comes in. HE is wearing the
    latest styles of the more up-market Italian designers.
    Bold but discreet is the theme. HE looks healthy, even
    rather sleek.*

*When he comes in, HE is holding several letters. Sitting in
a chair, HE opens each of the four, glances quickly
through them and when HE has finished, stands, goes
over to the desk, brings out a key ring and unlocks one
of the drawers and puts them in, locking up again.*

*There is a piece of paper in the typewriter carriage and HE
studies the typescript on it for awhile before going to
the kitchen area and, plugging in a kettle, picks up a
cafetière, then finds a jar full of coffee.*

*The cup he finds is made of a fine bone china. The sugar is
in cubes and there is a pair of silver tongs.*

*The point of this is to indicate his lifestyle has been raised
a few notches since we were last here.*

*While the water boils ADRIAN sits at the typewriter. HE
thinks, chin resting on his fists, then writes a few lines
rapidly.*

*A key turns in the door and SMYTHE comes in carrying a
brown bag of groceries. SHE holds a key which SHE
stuffs into her pocket as SHE closes the door, crosses to
the kitchen area and puts down the bag. SHE comes
over to ADRIAN and bends, looking over his shoulder
and reads what he has written.*

SMYTHE. How's it coming?
ADRIAN. All right. I had a good day.

(SHE takes off her coat and starts to put away the food.)

ADRIAN. What about you?
SMYTHE. So so. Do you mind pasta tonight?
ADRIAN. Fine.

SMYTHE. I found some linguine. I thought I'd make a tomato and basil sauce.

ADRIAN. What does "so so" mean?

(HE comes behind her and puts his arms around her waist. SHE leans her head back and rests it against his for a moment before HE lets her go and SHE continues filling the fridge.)

SMYTHE. Friday to most people means payday. To me, it means a gay priest with sexual hangups in the morning and two abandoned wives in the afternoon.

ADRIAN. Aren't there any clients that make you want to leap out of bed and race in to work?

SMYTHE. None these days. Maybe nostalgia is setting in, but there was a time when it was so much more *fun*! People came in with weird problems. Things you could really sink your teeth into.

ADRIAN. Like what?

(The water has boiled and HE is filling the cafetière.)

SMYTHE. I don't know—phobias. I like the challenge of a really good phobia. I once treated a woman who every night had to see her digital clock change from twenty-three fifty-nine to zero zero. If she didn't, she was convinced she would die the next day.

ADRIAN. Did you help her?

SMYTHE. I may have. I don't know. I don't know if I actually *care* anymore. Psychiatrists are like high court judges. For the first few years they practice, they're terrified of being wrong. For the next few years, they're convinced they're right. And for the rest of their lives, they don't give a shit either way. (*SHE has finished putting away the food, comes over and hugs him tightly.*) You know, so much of what you said was right! I process people. I don't cure them, just—give them a crutch for a while and pass them on. Now, I just want to shake them and say, "For God's sake, pull yourself together!" I think my days as an analyst are numbered.

ADRIAN. No, they aren't. Look at the job you've done on me—

(*HE grins, THEY separate and drink their coffee.*)

ADRIAN. I need some more advice. (*HE crosses to the typewriter and picks up some completed pages.*)

SMYTHE. Advice?

ADRIAN. I'm having trouble with Sophie. (*Sits on the bed, head against the wall and lays down each page as HE glances through them.*) Here's this woman who all her life has maintained that she has no interest in marriage or children, wedded to her career, who out of the blue falls in love with a younger man—

SMYTHE. (*SHE isn't surprised to hear this. In fact, SHE smiles as SHE lowers the coffee cup from her lips.*) Completely fictional, of course—

ADRIAN. (*HE smiles back, a kind of intimate conspiracy.*) Of course.

SMYTHE. Go on—

ADRIAN. She's had affairs, none of them fulfilling, most of them with married men. Through choice, mind you. That way she never has to face the prospect of a marriage proposal—

SMYTHE. Or even the prospect of sharing a flat—

ADRIAN. (*Makes a note on a piece of paper.*) Sophie is a woman who only looks for sex in the form of a zipless fuck.

SMYTHE. Come on, it's not *quite* as simple as that.

ADRIAN. (*Holds up the pages.*) As I'm finding out.

SMYTHE. I'm sure you are.

(*HE lays down the pages and comes over, stands behind her chair and loops his arms round her head gently, kissing her hair. SHE closes her eyes and brings her hands up to rest on his arms.*)

ADRIAN. You must be absolutely honest. Do you mind me writing about you like this?

SMYTHE. (*Shakes her head.*) No. As a matter of fact, it's quite therapeutic.

ADRIAN. Is there anything so far you object to?

SMYTHE. I'm not wild about the name Sophie—(*SHE looks up at him and diffuses the remark with a grin.*)

ADRIAN. (*HE lets her go and smiles. Now HE faces her, bending his knees to reach her level in the chair.*) You once said you lived in fear of someone asking to marry you—

SMYTHE. I've told you I'm Catholic. One of the old kind. I'd never agree to divorce. I could never stop thinking: "Suppose it doesn't work?" I couldn't bear to live the rest of my life in some kind of emotional prison.

ADRIAN. Being Catholic never stopped you having affairs with married men.

SMYTHE. No. Why should it? If Catholics thought
that way, there wouldn't be anyone in Italy who would take
their clothes off except to have a bath.

ADRIAN. You never wanted any of these lovers to
divorce their wives and marry you?

(A pause.)

SMYTHE. There was one—

ADRIAN. The one that lasted ten years?

SMYTHE. Yes. There was something special about
him, I suppose, to last that long. Anyway, he *didn't* ask
for a divorce, so that was that.

ADRIAN. In my story, Sophie's fallen in love for the
first time. My problem is, I think like a man. Men are
hopeless when it comes to romance.

SMYTHE. You said it.

ADRIAN. My first instinct is to have her say: "O my
darling, I never knew it could be like this, let's get married
right away!" But I have a feeling that's not *quite* right.

(SMYTHE laughs.)

ADRIAN. What are you laughing about?

SMYTHE. It *is* quite right, except nobody will admit
it.

ADRIAN. Admit what?

SMYTHE. That the most earnest desires are expressed
in such banal terms. The great majority of people think in
sentences no self-respecting novelist would ever write.
When they are in great emotional situations they use
simple language. "I just want to die!" "Will you always

love me for ever?" Put that in a book and you're a laughing
stock.
    ADRIAN. So do you think I should leave it just like
that? "O my darling, I never knew it could be like this,
let's get married right away?"
    SMYTHE. The truth is always simple. What you have
to do is dress it up a bit.
    ADRIAN. Lie?
    SMYTHE. If you like.

(A silence.)

    ADRIAN. The trouble is, I can't lie any more. You
cured me, remember?
    SMYTHE. *(Goes to the fridge and takes out an apple.)* I
taught you to control your fantasies. You can still lie, if
you have a mind to.
    ADRIAN. Except I think it's a bit like being an
alcoholic on the wagon. Tell just one fib—and I'm back
where I started.

*(SMYTHE takes a bite from the apple and offers him one.
    HE takes her wrist and nibbles at it.)*

    ADRIAN. You teach me to be truthful. I teach you to
eat fruit.
    SMYTHE. *(Looks around the room.)* And other things.
I've come to like things I only had contempt for.
Prettiness. Nice curtains, colors. You remember my office
when you first came—
    ADRIAN. There was a certain Stalinist influence—

SMYTHE. You should see it now. Eat your heart out, *Homes and Gardens.*
ADRIAN. And you've stopped smoking.
SMYTHE. I only smoked when I was under stress.
ADRIAN. When you lost control—
SMYTHE. I suppose so, yes.
ADRIAN. And you're in control now—
SMYTHE. I'm happy now.
ADRIAN. Someone can be a happy parasite.
SMYTHE. I don't particularly want to analyze *why* I'm happy. I just am.
ADRIAN. (*Comes towards her again, takes another bite of the apple.*) Good ...

(*HE picks up his typescript as SMYTHE goes to the sink and starts to prepare supper, putting on a large saucepan to boil, chopping tomatoes, garlic, etc.*
A silence continues for awhile. A mood of familiar, comfortable domesticity descends on the scene.
ADRIAN starts to write with a ball point as HE studies the typescript on the bed. When SHE glances across SHE sees him immersed in his work.)

SMYTHE. What are you writing?
ADRIAN. (*As HE writes.*) "I—don't—want—to— analyze why—I'm—happy. I—just—am."
SMYTHE. (*Smiles and continues chopping up the food.*) You like that?
ADRIAN. It fits.
SMYTHE. Have you decided how your story will end?
ADRIAN. I think so.
SMYTHE. How?

ADRIAN. Sophie will marry her bloke.

(A pause.)

SMYTHE. I hope it isn't just because you think a
novel has to end neatly.
ADRIAN. No—
SMYTHE. The trouble with real life is loose ends are
rarely tied and—worse—it goes on beyond the last page.
ADRIAN. Sophie will marry the man because they love
each other.
SMYTHE. Good.

*(ADRIAN looks across at SMYTHE busy at the sink. HE
lays down the papers, stands and crosses, takes her in
his arms from behind and holds her.)*

ADRIAN. I love you.
SMYTHE. *(SHE turns round in his arms.)* I know.
ADRIAN. I want to marry you.

*(SHE hesitates, gently disentangles herself from his arms
with a shy smile. SHE half-heartedly continues to
prepare the food.)*

ADRIAN. Well, Sophie says—
SMYTHE. I know what she says. You told me.
ADRIAN. Then why don't you—?
SMYTHE. *(Leaves the sink, moves towards the bed.)*
Has *she* mentioned the difference in their ages?
ADRIAN. No.
SMYTHE. She should.

ADRIAN. Why?

SMYTHE. Because it's important.

ADRIAN. (*Returns to his manuscript, picks up the pages and finds a place.*) "I love you," he whispered. "I want you to be my wife." She looked at him, her jaw dropping—" So here instead of saying, "O darling, I never knew it could be like this, 'let's get married right away."— you want her to answer: "But what about the difference in our ages—?"

SMYTHE. (*Gently takes the pages from his hands and lays them down.*) Let's forget the novel.

ADRIAN. All right—

SMYTHE. By the time you're forty, I'll be sixty.

ADRIAN. I *can* add up—

SMYTHE. Think about it.

ADRIAN. Why is age never a factor when older men want to marry young women—?

SMYTHE. Because a man of sixty can still look good. A woman just looks old.

ADRIAN. Not necessarily.

SMYTHE. At sixty, believe me, *I* will look old.

ADRIAN. Who cares about how we'll *look*?

SMYTHE. I will. Whenever the waiter hands me the bill in a restaurant, I'll care.

(*A pause.*)

ADRIAN. I have this theory. Do you want to hear it?

SMYTHE. What about?

ADRIAN. Since I've stopped telling lies, you've started.

SMYTHE. You think I'm lying?

ADRIAN. You don't love me.
SMYTHE. Yes, I do.
ADRIAN. Then marry me.

(A pause.)

ADRIAN. Q.E.D.
SMYTHE. Real life isn't a mathematical equation.
ADRIAN. The age difference has nothing to do with it.
You use it only as an excuse.
SMYTHE. Maybe.
ADRIAN. Why do you need an excuse?
SMYTHE. Why do you want to marry me?
ADRIAN. Because I can't imagine I'll ever want to
marry anyone else.
SMYTHE. Clients often fall in love with their
analysts. It's an occupational hazard.
ADRIAN. You mean this little scene is one you've
played before?
SMYTHE. No.
ADRIAN. You have a string of lovelorn patients
stretching back through the years—
SMYTHE. No.
ADRIAN. Then what do you mean?

(A silence.)

SMYTHE. *(Trying to find the words to say something
that has been on her mind for some time.)* I mean this. And
please don't misunderstand me. I actually *know* almost
nothing about you.
ADRIAN. You know enough to say you love me—

SMYTHE. Love doesn't need any information.
Marriage does.

ADRIAN. (*Shrugs and spreads his arms.*) Seek and ye
shall find. What do you want to know?

SMYTHE. During these past few months, whenever
I've come round here, I've never seen anything that tells
me about who you are, where you're from. Nothing. You
never mention your parents, whether you ever see them or
speak to them. I've never even seen a letter anywhere.
Most people have something stuck behind a vase on the
mantelpiece or lying around. But when I look around—
there's no clue about you at all.

ADRIAN. If you wanted to know anything, why didn't
you just ask?

SMYTHE. I tried to concentrate on the job in hand. I
wanted you to stop living in a world of make-believe.
Asking about you would have confused things. That's not
to say I didn't wonder. But before you straightened out, I
would never have known if you were lying or not. So—

ADRIAN. O.K. I've stopped fantasizing, right?

SMYTHE. I think so, yes.

ADRIAN. You want the truth?

SMYTHE. I'd like to hear *something*.

ADRIAN. There's no mystery. Letters—I've always
used a poste restante. Ever since my first few weeks here
when mail went missing. The postman shoves it through
the door on the ground floor and any of the half dozen
people living in this building can steal it. I lost a couple of
letters with checks in them so now I pick everything up at
the local post office.

SMYTHE. You read them there?

ADRIAN. Sometimes—

SMYTHE. And throw them away—?

ADRIAN. (*Looks at her a moment, goes to the desk and unlocks a drawer, takes out a handful from many letters inside and brandishes them.*) Do you want to read them—? They're nearly all bills—(*HE comes over and and holds them under her nose.*)

SMYTHE. No, of course not—

(*ADRIAN throws them on the bed.*)

ADRIAN. As for my parents—you know all about them.

SMYTHE. I know several versions. The last thing I heard was your father is an accountant—

ADRIAN. Sorry. That was a lie. I told you the truth about him the *first* time.

SMYTHE. About him being in the Secret Service?

ADRIAN. (*A smile.*) My father really is a spy.

(*This makes HER look very surprised.*)

ADRIAN. I really did grow up in Chelsea. My mother did have depressions. And I really do have a sister.

SMYTHE. (*Sits down, as if needing support.*) Then why haven't I met them? Have they ever been here to visit you? Telephoned—?

ADRIAN. Well, we haven't spoken in years.

SMYTHE. Why not?

(*A pause.*)

ADRIAN. You remember I told you about Anna?

SMYTHE. The randy Pole—

ADRIAN. (*Smiles.*) She *was* Polish, but she *wasn't* a nymphomaniac.

SMYTHE. What about her?

ADRIAN. I met her when I was seventeen. I'd gone to Warsaw on a school trip. This was in the pre-Glasnost days. She was staying in the same hotel. Six months later, she came to England.

SMYTHE. You were sleeping together—

ADRIAN. From day one. Maybe not in cinemas, but—

SMYTHE. All right—

ADRIAN. To cut a long and painful story short, my father came home one day and told me it had to end.

SMYTHE. Why?

ADRIAN. He said he'd been told by Foreign Office security that one of their suspects had been seen with his son.

SMYTHE. Anna was a *spy*—?

ADRIAN. Anna was a nineteen-year-old girl with no interest whatsoever in politics.

SMYTHE. What happened?

ADRIAN. I told my father there was no way I was going to stop seeing her just because some time-serving ex-copper on his staff said she was a security risk.

SMYTHE. So you carried on.

ADRIAN. For about a month.

SMYTHE. Then what happened?

ADRIAN. She wasn't there anymore.

SMYTHE. What do you mean?

ADRIAN. I mean, my father has her expelled.

SMYTHE. What—? (*SHE is dumbfounded.*)

ADRIAN. (*Reliving the experience and has both hands clenched by his sides. Slowly HE calms.*) We wrote to each other for awhile. That was the first time I used a poste restante. Then we stopped and I've no idea what happened to her. Probably got married. By this time I'd finished my A levels. I went off to college. Never went back home. Haven't spoken to my father since.

(*A long silence goes by.*)

SMYTHE. What about your mother—?

ADRIAN. My mother didn't come out of this well, either. She took his side, said didn't I realize with Daddy being in a sensitive job—it was never stated he was actually in the Secret Service, just—"something in the F.O."—didn't I realize that Anna was an embarrassment?

SMYTHE. Do you still love Anna?

ADRIAN. (*Shrugs.*) If you want the truth, I don't think I was ever really in love with her. We liked on another. She introduced me to sex. I'd never slept with a girl before Warsaw.

SMYTHE. You don't think there was a grain of truth in what your father said? A girl picks you up in a Polish hotel, immediately goes to bed with you—maybe they did know who your father was.

ADRIAN. Maybe. I don't know and I don't care. The fact is, he pulled a few strings and had her thrown out of the country because he was afraid I could tell her secrets. Christ, I wasn't even supposed to know he was a spook! (*A pause.*) It's often crossed my mind that maybe I inherited my compulsion to lie.

SMYTHE. Because it was your father's job to hide the truth doesn't make him a liar.

ADRIAN. What *is* lying but hiding the truth? Or being economical with it? Or any other fancy phrase they use to describe the work these people do? My father has been in the Secret Service since he left university. His entire life has been spent in dissemination. At one time he worked in a department whose only function was to misinform. To put stories into foreign newspapers to make hostile governments believe the wrong things! If that is your *job*, how do you manage your *life*?

(SMYTHE doesn't answer. SHE sees ADRIAN is in some distress and holds out her arm. HE takes her hand and SHE pulls him towards her and THEY embrace tightly.)

SMYTHE. Do you know what I think?

ADRIAN. What?

SMYTHE. I think you should try and patch things up.

(THEY move apart. SMYTHE sees the water is boiling and puts in the pasta while they speak.)

ADRIAN. Why?

SMYTHE. If I've learned anything from twenty years of hearing how people wreck their lives, it's to minimize hatred.

ADRIAN. To forgive my father is to condone what he did to Anna.

SMYTHE. So? You said you probably didn't love her. She was your introduction to sex. Thank you and goodbye.

It seems a bit strong to alienate your family for a bit of slap and tickle.

(THEY say nothing for some moments. SMYTHE finishes at the sink, wipes her hands on a tea towel and returns to her chair.
ADRIAN has found a bottle of wine, uncorked it and poured two glasses. HE hands one to her and THEY sip.)

ADRIAN. That sounds like good psychiatric advice, doctor.
SMYTHE. Think about it.

(A pause.)

ADRIAN. You've never had to tell lies, have you?
SMYTHE. I've never *had* to. But I have.
ADRIAN. When?
SMYTHE. I once said you were mad.
ADRIAN. *(Laughs.)* You're excused that one.
SMYTHE. You generally lie to other people. I've spent most of my life on my own. You *can* deceive yourself, but usually you aren't aware of it.
ADRIAN. These love affairs—
SMYTHE. Yes?
ADRIAN. The men had to lie all the time—
SMYTHE. Not necessarily—
ADRIAN. You mean they *told* their wives about you?
SMYTHE. *(Shows a moment's surprise. SHE hadn't realized this side of it.)* No ... What I meant was, they didn't lie to me.

ADRIAN. Didn't one of them say he was going to get a divorce?

SMYTHE. That was not so much a lie as a failure of courage.

ADRIAN. You believed him—

SMYTHE. Yes ... I don't know ... perhaps deep down I always suspected that he wouldn't.

ADRIAN. That he was not telling the truth?

SMYTHE. (*A smile.*) I'm delighted you have left your fantasy world behind. However, I didn't realize it would mean pursuing truth quite so vigorously—

ADRIAN. I'm sorry.

SMYTHE. You are right, of course—

ADRIAN. What about?

SMYTHE. My relationships *were* founded on a whole network of deception. I'd never thought about that before.

ADRIAN. But the one that lasted ten years—that's a long time to play charades.

SMYTHE. Yes.

ADRIAN. Why did it go on so long?

ADRIAN. Laziness, I suppose. And it fitted our schedules. We'd meet at my flat at one o'clock every Friday. I'd pick up a bag of bread and pate from Safeways and we'd eat and make love and be back at work by three. That allowed a short post coital nap. The timing was always exactly the same. We'd finish just before the Archers. I still can't hear that signature tune without feeling an overwhelming urge to go to sleep.

ADRIAN. That's all it was, a Friday bonk?

SMYTHE. We went abroad now and then. A long weekend to Paris or Amsterdam.

ADRIAN. What did he tell his wife?

SMYTHE. Oh, business—
ADRIAN. At weekends?
SMYTHE. He was a civil servant. He was involved in organizing international trade conventions. It was quite usual to meet at weekends. And his wife was American. She used to go back to the States to visit her relatives.
ADRIAN. Still, to go on for ten years! All that time keeping one half of your brain separate from the other. Rather like being a spy.
SMYTHE. I suppose.
ADRIAN. I couldn't do it.
SMYTHE. You've proved that.
ADRIAN. *(A grin.)* Yes. No two ways about me. Either the whole fantasy hog or nothing.

(SHE combs his hair with her fingers.)

ADRIAN. And his wife never suspected a thing—
SMYTHE. If she did, she didn't *do* anything about it. I thought *I* was meant to be asking about *you.*
ADRIAN. Do you still see him?
SMYTHE. No.
ADRIAN. Talk to him?
SMYTHE. Not any more.
ADRIAN. It's completely finished—
SMYTHE. Completely.
ADRIAN. So there is absolutely no reason at all why you can't marry me. *(A pause. Looks at her a long moment.)* Then you will—

(SHE doesn't answer, but SHE smiles.)

ADRIAN. Don't go home tonight.

SMYTHE. (*Looks at the single bed.*) We'll never fit into *that*—

ADRIAN. We can sleep on the floor.

SMYTHE. It's still a single mattress!

ADRIAN. I want you to stay.

SMYTHE. I suppose it's time I told you something.

ADRIAN. You're a man—

SMYTHE. No.

ADRIAN. What?

SMYTHE. I'm not very good at sex.

ADRIAN. Nor am I. We can practice on each other.

SMYTHE. (*Laughs.*) I mean it. I'm not. I'm very passive.

(*ADRIAN holds out his hand. SHE takes it and HE pulls her gently from her chair. HE leads her past the stove where HE turns off the gas under the boiling saucepan full of spaghetti, then towards the bed. HE bends, picks her up and lays her down on the bed. HE squeezes down beside her in the crumpled space.*)

SMYTHE. You're not going to enjoy this, I promise you—

ADRIAN. Be quiet. Now *I'm* the analyst—(*HE takes her shoes off.*)

(*SHE subsides into giggles until SHE is silent.*)

ADRIAN. Ready?

SMYTHE. (*Suppressing a smile.*) Ready.

ADRIAN. You say you've not done this before—

SMYTHE. Not for some time—

ADRIAN. You may feel a little self-conscious at first but that will soon pass. (*A pause.*) You say "I want to cooperate, I really do."

SMYTHE. What—?

ADRIAN. Remember how my first session started?

SMYTHE. (*Smiling.*) Ah—yes—I want to cooperate. I really do—

ADRIAN. (*Smiling.*) You're not here to cooperate. You're here to make spontaneous love.

SMYTHE. Right. I mean, fine ... I mean O.K. ... I mean "Ready when you are, Mr. DeMille."

(HE leans over, takes her in his arms and kisses her tenderly as the CURTAIN FALLS.)

ACT II

Scene 2

The same, two week later.

The room is empty. After a few moments, two pairs of FEET can be heard mounting the stairs outside the door rapidly. A KEY turns in the lock and ADRIAN and SMYTHE come in.

SMYTHE is in a smart daytime suit, ADRIAN in a good suit with a tie, and carnation in his buttonhole. Both of them have bits of confetti on their clothes and in their hair.

*THEY are in high spirits, happy and boisterous. At the
door ADRIAN drags SMYTHE back onto the landing.*

ADRIAN. Whoops—come back—

*(HE reappears carrying her in his arms, making a point of
stepping over the threshold. SHE laughs and hugs his
neck. We haven't seen her like this before. Almost
kittenish.
HE carries her to the bed, a cross between Tarzan and
Frankenstein's monster, and drops her onto the bed.
Then HE pounds his chest, gorilla-style.)*

ADRIAN. Now we mate! *(Whipping off his jacket and
yanking at his tie.)*
SMYTHE. *(Still laughing wildly.)* Say please!
ADRIAN. I don't have to anymore. You're my wife ...

*(HE becomes gentle, loses the gorilla, lowers himself and
kisses her very tenderly. HE almost falls off the edge of
the bed.)*

ADRIAN. Now it's official, we're going to need a
bigger bed.
SMYTHE. Why? So you'll have room to move away
from me?

*(SHE rolls over on top of him, grabs his hair and kisses
him hard.)*

ADRIAN. You are an unmitigated liar.
SMYTHE. I am? Why?

ADRIAN. You said you were no good at this sort of thing.

(SHE smiles.)

ADRIAN. *(Rubs confetti from her hair.)* Sally did a thorough job with the confetti.
SMYTHE. *(Stands.)* She seemed to hit it off with Carlos.
ADRIAN. Now she's probably *having* it off with Carlos—

(HE puts a finger out and points to the floor as HE stands and takes a bottle of champagne from the fridge.)

SMYTHE. *(Taking out some telegrams from her pocket.)* A telegram from my parents.
ADRIAN. What does it say?
SMYTHE. *(Reads.)* "Finally. Mother."
ADRIAN. Neat.

(HE is opening and pouring the champagne. SHE looks at another.)

SMYTHE. My brother in Kenya ... *(Another.)* Uncle Roger— *(Reads.)* "As a dedicated pederast, I heartily applaud your choice of a younger man—"
ADRIAN. Uncle Roger sounds all right—
SMYTHE. He's actually got five children from three marriages, but he likes to brighten up the lives of British Telecom.

(SHE takes a glass and THEY clink rims.)

ADRIAN. (*Bogart.*) "Here's looking at you, Mrs. Wainwright—"

(THEY drink, eyes locked a moment.)

SMYTHE. (*Turns and looks round the room.*) I don't see anything from your family.
ADRIAN. I have a poste restante, remember?
SMYTHE. But you *did* phone them?
ADRIAN. I talked to my mother.
SMYTHE. What did she say?
ADRIAN. She wanted to come, but she understood why we didn't want any fuss.
SMYTHE. Why *you* didn't want any.
ADRIAN. Why *I* didn't.
SMYTHE. And your father?
ADRIAN. I've no intention of speaking to him again. Ever.
SMYTHE. Isn't that going to be rather difficult? Are we going to spend the rest of our lives dodging round corners whenever he turns up?

(SHE sees HE is ill at ease, fiddles with the stem of his glass, avoiding her eyes.)

SMYTHE. Well—*are* we?

(SHE comes over to him and forces HIM to meet her gaze.)

SMYTHE. Don't you think the time has come to forgive him?

(There is another lengthy pause. SHE is alarmed to find ADRIAN deliberately looking away, unusually hesitant and withdrawn.)

SMYTHE. What's the matter? Tell me.
ADRIAN. You—er—you might want to put that glass down.
SMYTHE. Don't patronize me. You have something to say, say it.
ADRIAN. You know I told you my mother got depressed.
SMYTHE. Yes—
ADRIAN. Well, I wasn't the cause. There was no Empty Nest Syndrome, nothing like that. The trouble started much earlier. Soon after she was married.
SMYTHE. Why? What was the trouble?
ADRIAN. *(It takes him a few seconds to frame his words.)* My mother found out she was unable to have children.
SMYTHE. *(Reacts sharply.) What*—?
ADRIAN. They tried, but when nothing happened, she had some tests. It was her problem not his.
SMYTHE. You were *adopted?*
ADRIAN. Yes.

(The glass spills in her hand a little and SHE puts it down.)

SMYTHE. Why didn't you tell me this before?

ADRIAN. (*Continues as if HE doesn't hear her.*) She told me when I was quite young. And my sister. It didn't make any difference. We'd been adopted at birth. She was the only mother we knew.

SMYTHE. I can't understand why you've never mentioned this before—

ADRIAN. You will—

(This makes HER look alarmed, but HE takes her hand a moment before letting it go and continuing.)

ADRIAN. Then they changed the law and made it possible to trace natural parents.

SMYTHE. And you did?

ADRIAN. Mine lived in Canada. Quebec. She ran her own business. She never married. (*HE goes to his desk and brings out a piece of paper.*)

SMYTHE. How did you feel towards her?

ADRIAN. Like I'd feel towards any stranger. The one thing she did, though, was to give me my original birth certificate. She'd kept it all these years.

SMYTHE. (*Looks at it.*) There a Raymond Wainwright down as the father—

ADRIAN. She filled in a name. To make it look respectable.

SMYTHE. Did she say who your father was?

ADRIAN. Eventually. It took a few hangovers. She had a bit of a drink problem, and I was only eighteen at the time.

SMYTHE. So you traced him as well—

ADRIAN. I didn't have to.

(A moment passes while SHE tries to work this out. But SHE can't.)

SMYTHE. What are you saying?

ADRIAN. I'm saying my father is my real father. This woman had a child by him. He adopted it. The child was me. Five years later he did the same thing with another woman and got my sister.

SMYTHE. *(Still takes a moment to work it out.)* They were surrogate mothers.

ADRIAN. If you like.

SMYTHE. All right ... it's unorthodox. But it's not illegal. Your mother agreed to it, presumably—

ADRIAN. She had no idea who the mothers were. She simply got us from an adoption agency.

SMYTHE. Wait. She didn't *know*—?

ADRIAN. She still doesn't.

SMYTHE. You never told anyone what you had found out?

ADRIAN. No one. Not even my sister. Only you.

SMYTHE. Why not?

ADRIAN. What would have been the point? She grew out of her depressions. She loved us. She's had a happy life.

SMYTHE. Provided by her husband who you profess to hate.

ADRIAN. You might say that.

ADRIAN. I *am* saying that. Any other man might well have asked for a divorce and looked for another wife who *could* give him a family.

ADRIAN. *(Gives a short laugh.)* He would never have left her.

SMYTHE. Because he loved her so much—

ADRIAN. Because she was so *rich*! The only reason he married her was on account of the five million dollars she inherited when she came of age. Who do you think pays for everything? The house in London, the country estate. His clubs, his horses. Not the Secret Service. His salary as an aging spy wouldn't even keep him in cigars. Do you think he'd leave all that for the sake of begetting a few kids? My father would rather stay married to Lucretia Borgia, than wind up in a bedsitter on the Earls Court Road.

(A pause. Something he said has made SMYTHE uneasy. A chord strikes somewhere deep inside.)

SMYTHE. She inherited five million—dollars?
ADRIAN. Yes.
SMYTHE. Your mother's American?
ADRIAN. Yes.
SMYTHE. You never told me that before, either.
ADRIAN. No. I didn't.

(HE comes over and holds her but SHE pulls away, growing alarmed, anxious, confused. HE holds her firmly and makes HER look at him.)

ADRIAN. The woman in Canada told me something else. When I asked her how come she didn't have an abortion, she said she was Catholic. When I asked her why she didn't keep her baby, she said she was building up her business. She didn't have the time. And when I asked her why she didn't get married, she said she wasn't interested in sharing her life with anyone—

SMYTHE. Let me go!

ADRIAN. (*Holds on.*) And guess what? My sister's mother fitted exactly the same pattern. She slept with my father for almost twelve years. My father has had three affairs that have lasted his entire marriage—

(*Now HE has HER eyes locked into his.*)

ADRIAN. *Three* affairs, Julia. I have *two* sisters. The youngest is just eight. I traced her mother too.

(*Gradually SMYTHE stops struggling and HE lets her go. SHE stands there, motionless.*)

SMYTHE. Your father's name is Charles Barton.

ADRIAN. He is a spy. He works under several covers. One of them is an organizer of international trade conventions.

SMYTHE. I did have a child. Two years after we met. It was a mistake.

ADRIAN. The others said the same. Mistakes that *he* arranged to happen.

SMYTHE. He said it was all right. He knew a good adoption agency.

ADRIAN. He certainly did. God knows how much he paid them to bend the rules.

SMYTHE. And there was no question of an abortion. So—he *selected* me for my special qualities. Like a prize heifer.

ADRIAN. He deceived you. He deceived the others. And for twenty-five years, he deceived my mother. And you want me to minimize hatred—?

SMYTHE. He often spoke about his children. A boy, James—who went off to America—

ADRIAN. My adopted name is James Barton—

SMYTHE. —Clare and Emma. I had no *idea*—n o reason to think that Emma was mine!

ADRIAN. After he expelled Anna, I went off to the States. My mother came over to see me but he and I haven't spoken since.

SMYTHE. And you never told him what you'd found out.

ADRIAN. No.

SMYTHE. (*Moves away, her voice hardening.*) But now you're going to, I suppose.

ADRIAN. I'll never say anything. Not while my mother's still alive.

SMYTHE. You bastard! It wasn't enough to find me. You wanted total humiliation! You wanted to smash me into pieces! The fun you had!

ADRIAN. Not now—it's different now!

SMYTHE. You can stop lying! It's all over. The job's done! There's no need for any more fantasies! Any more games! You got me to marry you! The humiliation is complete!

(*SHE pummels him as hard as she can on his body and HE dodges her flailing fists going for his face. HE catches her wrists and THEY struggle. SHE uses her feet, kicks him but HE hangs on until THEY fall onto the bed where HE smothers her struggles and puts a hand over her mouth. HE is out of breath.*)

ADRIAN. That—that was true at first! I hated you so
much! You—you'd slept with him—for ten years! You
never gave a thought to the fact he had a wife! When I
found out you were a shrink, I thought—what the hell,
let's,have some fun before we let it all out. I wanted to
give you pain! But then you began to hit back the second
time I came round. I said to myself—hey, there's a bit
more mileage in this. I know—fake a suicide and *really*
make her feel guilty! You were absolutely hooked!

*(SHE muffles a cry and struggles but HE keeps his hand
over her mouth.)*

ADRIAN. Then everything changed. As time went on, I
thought less about why I was doing this. And more about
you. I saw you were just one more victim of my father. I
wasn't amusing myself anymore. Each time you came
round here, I felt more and more ashamed at what was
happening. So I stopped. I stopped hating you. I started to
love you. You can leave. I won't blame you, but I'd like
you to go knowing that I'm finally telling the whole,
uncontaminated truth. I love you.

*(SMYTHE has stopped struggling. ADRIAN slowly takes
away his hand and SHE is silent. HE stands and SHE
follows, calmly smoothing down her dress.)*

SMYTHE. Thank you. I'll take that thought with me.
But I'd like to leave something as well.

*(SHE is calm, even smiling. Then SHE brings back her
arm and hits him. This can be a slap to the face. I prefer*

a full-blooded fist to the chin myself, nothing sissy, but whatever come naturally. Either way it sends ADRIAN staggering back, dazed.
Then SMYTHE leaves.
ADRIAN shakes his head to clear it. HE looks at the door, resigned. Then sits heavily in a chair, holding his head in his hands. When he takes them away he looks in total despair. HE stands and looks at his reflection in a wall mirror.)

ADRIAN. (*To himself.*) You total arsehole ... (*HE takes the champagne bottle and drinks from the neck but slams it down and bursts into tears. Standing forlornly, HE begins to weep, his body shaking, his eyes closed.*

(*SMYTHE returns. SHE stands watching him. Finally HE opens his eyes and sees her.*)

SMYTHE. You always meant to keep everything from your mother. That's what you said, wasn't it? (*HE nods.*) Then marrying me wasn't so smart, was it?
ADRIAN. No.
SMYTHE. After all, you could never guarantee I wouldn't tell her, could you?
ADRIAN. No.
SMYTHE. Better if I'd just served your humorous purposes and disappeared.
ADRIAN. Yes.
SMYTHE. (*Comes towards him.*) Yes. So this ring (*Holds up her finger.*)—might just be for real.
ADRIAN. Could be.

SMYTHE. (*Wipes a tear from his cheek.*) I wonder if these are real too.

ADRIAN. There's only one way to find out.

SMYTHE. (*Takes him into her arms.*) I'm still not sure.

ADRIAN. Nor am I.

SMYTHE. I suppose I have to do something else I've never done before.

ADRIAN. What?

SMYTHE. I suppose I have to take a chance. (*A pause. SHE comes away.*) Have you given any thought to what will happen when you take me home to meet Daddy?

ADRIAN. Not after the massive coronary, no.

SMYTHE. Oh no! That would be awful. No, I hope your father lives to be a hundred.

ADRIAN. You do—? Why?

SMYTHE. Well, while I was storming down those stairs a minute ago, swearing never to come back, something occurred to me.

ADRIAN. What was that?

SMYTHE. You said he's entirely dependent on your mother for money.

ADRIAN. Completely.

SMYTHE. Then think of it. Once he sees his new daughter-in-law, once he realizes we aren't going to blow his cover, if that's the right term, he's going to start walking on eggs. When he sees me speaking to your mother, he'll worry about what I'm saying to her. You might drag Canada into the dinner conversation. We'll look at him with a curious, half mocking smile. Then we'll raise an eyebrow. He'll choke on his port at the mere mention of Amsterdam or Paris. I need only take Emma on my knee and he'll feel that constriction over his heart that will send his pulse racing whenever there's a family gathering. All his lies, all his cheating, all his deceptions will hang slowly twisting in the air. Every night he'll wake up bathed in sweat because he'll never be able to answer the one perpetual question that torments his brain: Will they tell her? I'd be very surprised if he has one moment's peace for the rest of his, I hope, extremely long life.

ADRIAN. (*Has gradually developed a smile of utter admiration and awe.*) Where did you learn to be so cruel?

SMYTHE. Oh, I was taught by experts. (*Holding his look.*)

ADRIAN. (*Eventually reaches for the telephone and starts to dial.*) You were right.

SMYTHE. What are you doing?

ADRIAN. It's time to minimize hatred—(*Into phone.*) Charles Barton, please—this is his son— (*As HE waits HE exchanges a smile.*)

SMYTHE. Good.

ADRIAN. From now on, I intend to take your advice to the letter—(*Into phone.*) Hello, Father ... yes, it has, a long time. But I hope we can put that behind us now ... Good ... Yes, that's right, I got married this morning ... why—er—yes—we'd love to come down to the country tonight—

SMYTHE. (*Alarmed.*) Oh no! Not yet, I'm not ready for it yet!

ADRIAN. (*Grinning broadly.*) Look, er, Father, my wife is dying to introduce herself—

SMYTHE. No!!

ADRIAN. She's right here ...

(HE holds the receiver out ar arm's length toward Smythe. At first SHE remains frozen to the spot. But gradually SHE comes forward, starts to smile at Adrian. HE takes her other hand as SHE collects the receiver.)

SMYTHE. Hello ... yes ... Well, actually I met your son when he came to my consulting rooms ... I'm a psychiatrist. My name? It's Julia. Why yes, that's right. Julia Smythe ...

(The stage LIGHTS start to dim.)

SMYTHE. Hello? Hello? Are you still there? Hello ... hello ...

(The stage goes DARK.)

End of Play

A Note About Costumes and Properties

Smythe changes her smart office suits in the three scenes of Act I, although in the third scene she never removes her topcoat. During the second act, she wears more casual wear. Adrian is required to look different between scenes one and two merely by a change of clothes. Smythe uses a watch with a timer alarm. Adrian produces a pocket-sized recording machine that reproduces a short conversation between them. In Act II, he uses a typewriter. The kitchen needs a plug to heat water in a kettle. Coffee is drunk from mugs. Later some food is prepared but not cooked in the kitchen area. Adrian produces an official birth certificate at one point and in the last scene of the play, both are required to be sprinkled with confetti, or rice. Smythe picks up a book which the audience might see has a cover with the words: "The Movie Quote Book" written large. A couple of other large volumes should be in the bookcase beside the hi-fi. A bowl of fresh fruit, apples in particular, feature in the second act. Smythe prepares a spaghetti sauce of fresh tomatoes and either basil leaves or parsley. Now and again they open wine or champagne. Smythe occasionally smokes.

Ground Plan

There are two locations in the play. The first is a psychiatrist's consulting room which is represented by the stage right portion of the ground plan. During the first three scenes the kitchen area, upstage left entrance, hi-fi, etc. are screened off. The reclining couch doubles as the bed. At the end of the third scene of Act I, the screen is removed, the couch moved to form the bed and the desk and chair screened. Now we have the second location, a small apartment. This scene change takes about three minutes.

During the interval, the apartment remains the location, but it becomes considerably smarter. Bright curtains are placed over the upstage window, the bed receives a duvet, the table becomes a working top for a typewriter and the kitchen area looks cleaner. All exits and entrances take place through the upstage left door, which has also been repaired.

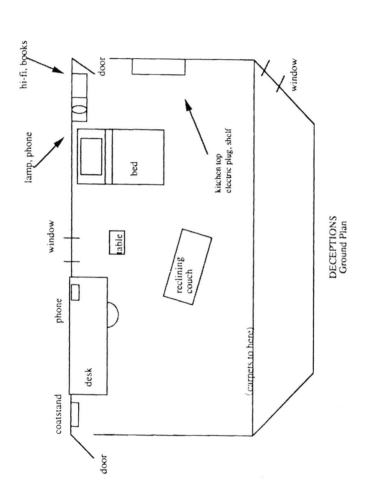

hi-fi, books

door

lamp, phone

window

phone

coatstand

door

desk

table

reclining couch

bed

kitchen top
electric plug, shelf

window

(carpets to here)

DECEPTIONS
Ground Plan